5.   Afterward

The Good Mudder's Guide
A Manual For Horse Show Mothers

Foreword

I AM PROUD and pleased to have been asked to write the Foreword to this book, THE GOOD MUDDERS' GUIDE. I have been privileged to be a *Horse Show Mother* for a number of years now. The experience has been a lot of fun. It has also been frustrating, nerve-racking, sometimes boring, sometimes definitely not boring, freezing cold, roasting hot, a time of incredible highs, many lows and a lot of in-betweens.

My two daughters and I are usually chief groomers, braiders and muckers. I am also in charge of hoof dressing, so I can say from experience that the situations described in THE GOOD MUDDERS' GUIDE really do happen and are absolutely true. I am usually cast in the role of trainer as well, so I don't have anyone to blame when things go wrong either.

We have had a lot of fun as a family from the world of horses and ponies. I wouldn't trade in those experiences for anything. I do admit, however, that on a cold, snowy evening in January, when the ponies have found ingenious new ways to misbehave, and there are "umpteen" classes before we can go home, the "fun" is very hard to find. On the other hand, there is nothing better than a warm spring day at a nice show with ponies properly cleaned and braided and behaving.

Horse Show Mother is a title that carries with it a responsibility to support and encourage your child as much as possible. One can only do this by knowing something about the sport.

THE GOOD MUDDERS' GUIDE is certainly a painless point from which to start; it covers everything a beginning mother needs to know and then some in a "user friendly" and humorous manner. It could easily be a basic handbook for the new *Horse Show Mother*, a great topic of conversation between classes, or an enjoyable brush-up for the experienced Horse Show Mother. I'm sure even the young riders will enjoy the apt cartoons and drawings.

To the uninitiated, a big horse show in full swing can be pretty overwhelming, especially if one is not familiar with which end of the pony to hold on to, much less lead around. As with any sport, if you know something about it, watching becomes more enjoyable.

Happiness is indeed a full can of hoof dressing!

MARY CHAPOT

Mary Chapot is a most highly-respected personality in the horse show world. A member of the United States Equestrian Team for 10 years, she competed for the United States in the 1964 and 1968 Olympics and participated in two Pan American Games During the 1963 Pan American Games she was an Individual Gold Medalist and has won 10 Grand Prix. Mrs. Chapot is an AHSA judge and has officiated at all hunt seat finals at one time or another. With her husband Frank, she owns and operates a breeding and training farm in New Jersey. For 1987, her 17-year-old daughter, Wendy won the Ruth O'Keefe Meredith Award as best Junior Horse Person of the Year. Wendy's 15-year-old sister Laura has also made her presence felt in the horse show world. Among Laura's achievements is the Grand Pony Hunter Championship at the AHSA Pony finals for 1987.

"Some days it rains . . ."

Acknowledgements

THE FOLLOWING people gave their time, advice and encouragement. It is our pleasure to thank them (though none of us can take responsibility for a technique or product not working as described). Naomi Blumenthal, Linda Burke, Custer Cassidy, Mary Chapot, Erin Cunningham, Gary Duffy & Asbury Hill Farm, Brigid Flanigan, Ray and Janet Herhold & Hobby Horse Farm, Peg Hull, Lynn Jacobs, Diane King, Sarah King, Susan Lowe & If Only Farm, Matthew Martin, Nicole Martin, Fred Metcalf, Kay Metcalf, Kate Seaver, Sydney Seaver, Ethel Titchener, Lewis Trumble, Nancy Trumble, and all of the Horse Show Mothers and Horse Show Fathers who contributed to this book. The excerpts from the AHSA Rule Book were reproduced with the persmission of the American Horse Shows Association, Inc.; we thank them for their help.

A well-dressed Horse Show Mother

Introduction

J UST AS THERE IS a recognized breed called *stage mothers*, there is also a class fondly referred to (at least some of the time) as *Horse Show Mothers (HSMs)*. It is our contention that horse shows would grind to a halt without the behind-the-scenes help of the HSMs — or at least stumble along at an uneven pace. In addition, HSMs are famous enough to have been referred to in novels about the horse show world, to have mugs inscribed to them, and have jokes made about them. However, until now they haven't been taken seriously enough to have a book written especially for them.

HSMs are not always clear about how they found their calling. Some rode and showed as children; they understood the show world and became HSMs naturally. Their children, being around horses and instructors, learned to ride — almost, it appears — by osmosis.

Other women, admitting to childhood dreams of owning a pony themselves, were only too willing to give their own children the chance to ride and compete. There are also HSMs who could not figure out where this inconvenient and demanding love of horses came from. They shook their heads, grumbled with the rest of us, and learned more about horses than they ever wanted to know. Chances are no one ever asked these HSMs if they had an aptitude for horse show motherhood, i.e. if they:

Made lists.

Saved old towels.

Owned a pair of knee-high rubber boots or L.L. Bean duckies.

Liked animals and children.

Were good losers.

Enjoyed seeing the sun rise . . . and set.

Liked fresh air and fast food (the latter is the only thing fast at a horse show).

Chances are they became involved by default, as we did. Our children began riding lessons. They improved. We leased ponies so that they could ride between lessons. They improved. They outgrew the leased ponies. The trainer suggested that it was time to buy ponies and we found ourselves

15

Passing time productively

A Horse Show Mother at the ring with children, ponies, grooming kit and ribbons

16

considering how much money to spend and convincing our husbands (who said "Never.") that now it was appropriate to get the children their own ponies.

We hunted for the best animals for the money and found them: one aged pony with lots of experience who simply trotted off with many blue ribbons that first summer at the local unrated shows; and two green (i.e. inexperienced) ponies with potential for A shows. Before we knew what we were doing, we were at our first A show and the children were winning ribbons. The ribbons were a delightful surprise as was the small amount of prize money. There were other surprises connected with going to shows, some of them less than delightful and a consequence of the fact that we were HSMs who knew next to nothing about ponies, shows, trainers, etc.

When we became new mothers we found countless books to help us through the feelings of quiet desperation, total responsibility, and absolute exhaustion. There was advice on how to deal with physical symptoms, advice on emotional growth, advice on picking nursery schools, and advice on toys and games. Advice was available on practically everything about children we could think of.

When we became new HSMs we found countless books on riding, showing, caring for ponies, breeding, shoeing, training, jumping, dressage — everything about horses and riding but one. There were no books on coping with the feelings of quiet desperation, total responsibility, and absolute exhaustion that earmark new horse show motherhood; no advice was available on coping with the unique combination of child, pony, tack, trainer and show that confront the HSM. In fact, in the beginning the extent of our ignorance was such that we didn't even know how much we didn't know and therefore how much we had to learn.

Now we hope that the things we found will help others about to embark on this sometimes perilous, often illogical, and almost always fun world of the horse show, the horse, the rider, and if the rider is under 18 — the HSM.

We are not yet experts (though daily we are becoming more knowledgeable, as the reader will). In fact, in our non-expertise lies our special qualification for writing this book. The HSM is not an expert but, of her, much expertise is expected. We felt that the time was ripe for us to put down in words our observations before we too look as if we are born to the barn, the stall, the tack and the horse; before we talk as if we understand the difference between *picking out a stall* (i.e. choosing a stall) and *picking out a stall* (i.e. picking out manure from a stall) and know without thinking that *she pinned* means that she received a ribbon. Having found no Dr. Spock, we decided to write a book for the green (i.e. inexperienced) HSM.

The book is organized chronologically: we walk the new HSM through her first horse show from pre-registration to understanding the classes and how they are judged. We cover what the HSM needs to know about forms,

17

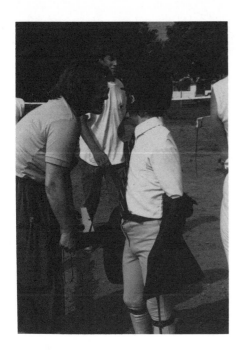

Time out for encouragement

A Horse Show Mother
cleaning a girth

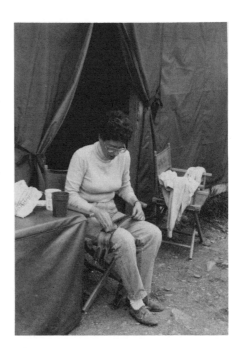

classes, and prizes; proper attire for the child and pony (and incidentally for herself); about physically helping her child with the animal; and how she (the HSM) can all the while maintain her sanity.

Since our experience so far encompasses only ponies, we talk about them instead of horses. Most of it, however, does overlap and apply to horses. And while we recognize that children, trainers, judges, and even farriers are both male and female, we adopted a single gender to describe each.

We urge the reader to consider the positives of horse shows:

Horse shows are good for losing weight; you are far too busy following orders to find the food stand.

Horse shows are good for gaining weight; you make many trips to food stands for the kids, why not indulge in a sandwich, salad, and sundae.

Horse shows are good for getting a tan; forego a hat and enjoy the hot sun beating down on the shadeless ringside.

Horse shows are good for hydrating your complexion. At some shows it rains — it rains the first day, it rains the second day, it rains the third day.

Horse shows are good for watching and listening to people.

Horse shows are good for being watched and listened to. A good thing to bear in mind is that eccentricity is acceptable and kindness always wins out over vindictiveness.

HSMs are permitted to attend exhibitors' parties.

HSMs have the opportunity to drive long distances to interesting county fairs.

HSMs can learn new skills: braiding, grooming, saddling, etc.

Horse shows are good places for acquiring a taste for exotic new drinks like warm, undiluted bourbon in lavatory paper cups.

All this is in addition to the benefits your child gains from working with and assuming responsibility for an animal, and from competition. Besides, we found horse shows to be fun.

And, finally, we admit that this book was a way to put our knowledge, all those hours of laughter, tension, tears, sweat and learning to some use; a way to prolong a summer's fun while we prepare for the new show season.

The end of a long day

The reward at the end of the end of a long day

1

The Prize List — Your Official Guide to a Horse Show

Mother's Aid

Carry your copy of the Prize List in a brown paper bag. If no one knows you have a copy, no one will want to borrow it. And if no one borrows it, then no one will lose it.

IN THE BEGINNING we discovered that the schedule of events (what most people would call a program) was referred to in the show world as the Prize List. It made little sense to us at the time, but it was filed away as a bit of jargon that set apart those in the know. No longer being green HSMs, we know that in some classes there are prizes of money (called *payback*) and therein, we suspect, lies the reason for the name.

Just as it was our first bit of horse show jargon, so the Prize List will be the HSM's first real contact with a rated show, and obtaining a copy may be the first challenge she faces. (We deal here with rated shows in which entries are usually mailed in ahead. However, at local unrated ones in which she signs up the day of the show, the Prize List is also the first thing to get hold of, and the one thing to hang on to, in addition to hope and her sense of humor.) The HSM can ask around the barn for copies, always being sure to check the bulletin board. Tack shops often have Prize Lists for local shows available. The AHSA (American Horse Show Association) magazine, *Horse Show*, routinely pubishes the schedule for the upcoming year of AHSA-recognized shows, including the address and phone number of the show secretary whom you can contact for a copy of the Prize List. We discovered that our names quickly found their way onto several mailing lists and consequently Prize Lists are now routinely mailed to our homes.

"To err is human; to judge divine"

Mother's Aid

Save the Prize Lists. Old ones have a phone number to call for this year's copy.

For a guide to a horse show you need look no further than the Prize List.

Mother's Aid

If, after looking at the Prize List, you have questions, you can always call a show secretary . . . We have found them unfailingly polite and helpful.

The Prize List contains:

Directions to the Show Grounds

These are invaluable because sometimes horse shows are hard to find, children are even harder to subdue if they think they're late, and it is no fun to backtrack when you're hauling ponies. We know of one HSM who missed a turn and since she was unable to back up while hauling a trailer had to drive five miles before finding a parking lot large enough to turn around in. The mother missed her turn — the child missed her first class.

We discovered that one true test of a marriage is to put your spouse behind the wheel of a vehicle pulling a loaded two-horse trailer and then ask him to turn around in someone's driveway because you turned left at the light when you should have turned right.

A List of the Officials of the Show

This includes not only the judge, steward, course designer (after all, you want to know whom to be mad at when your child goes off course) and announcer, but also the farrier (the person who shoes the pony) and veterinarian. Should you have a problem you know who's *on call.*

Overheard — HSM to HSM: "I don't like this judge. Let's remember his name . . . What is his name anyway?"

A Listing of the Divisions and If They're Rated

The AHSA is the national organization which regulates horse shows in the United States. Horse shows can be either rated or unrated. Rated shows are divided into *A3, A2, A1, B* and *C* levels. Generally speaking, the competition is toughest at the *A3* level — the prize money is higher, more

23

The indispensable farrier

The ringmaster

"Please don't wrinkle my ribbons."

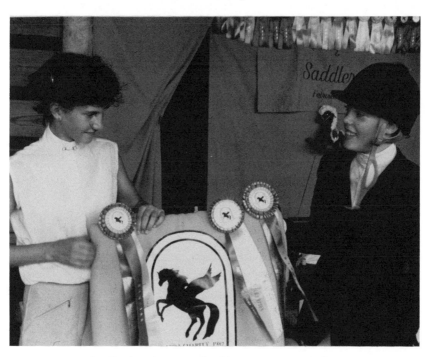

Inscribed coolers are prized by young competitors

classes are held, the points for classes are higher, and the show lasts for several days.

A show can be rated *A* in one division and *B* in another; in these cases the prize money and points depend on the classification of the division. A division may be rated by both the AHSA and other organizations which give year-end awards. The Prize List states which divisions count toward high point awards offered by various organizations and qualify the pony or rider for further competition.

There are also many local shows which are unrated by the AHSA. Although a competitor cannot earn points that count towards AHSA awards, he or she may earn points toward local year-end awards. These shows can be a lot of fun and give the children and ponies *mileage*, i.e. experience.

Entry Fees

The entry fee for each class or division will be clearly stated in the Prize List. The closing date for entries can be found here also. Post entries are those made after the official closing date. If post entries are accepted, the fees are generally higher.

Awards

The Prize List includes information about the awards. For instance, if it says *trophy and six ribbons*, this means that first place will be awarded a trophy and a blue ribbon while second through sixth places will be awarded (respectively) red, yellow, white, pink and green ribbons. *Trophy* can refer to a cooler, silver bowl, plate, fly sheet, etc. In England and Canada first place is awarded a red ribbon and second a blue.

Mother's Aid
Make note on the back of the ribbon who won it and for what class. This helps resolve disputes at the end of the day as to which ribbons belong to which child.

Suppose the Prize List says, "Returns $20, $15, $10 and $8." This means that first place will receive $20 in prize money while second through fourth receive $15, $10, and $8.

Warning — We found that while it is possible to *win* money at horse shows it is next to impossible to *make* money at horse shows.

26

6:30-8:00 a.m. - Unjudged Warm-up
8:00 a.m.

17. AHSA Pony Medal
48. Small Pony
49. Small Pony Conformation
50. Small Pony
52. Medium Pony
53. Medium Pony Conformation
54. Medium Pony
56. Large Pony
57. Large Pony Conformation
58. Large Pony
55. Large Pony Conformation U/S
47. Small Pony Conformation U/S
51. Medium Pony Conformation U/S
77. NEHC Pleasure
62. Schooling Hunter Under Saddle
59. Children's U/S
 1. Maiden Flat
 3. Novice Flat
74. Short Stirrup Flat
 5. Limit Flat
63. Schooling Hunter
64. Schooling Hunter
 2. Maiden Fences
 4. Novice Fences
 6. Limit Fences

60. Children's Hunter
61. Children's Hunter
75. Short Stirrup Equitation
76. Short Stirrup Equitation Championship
11. Open Equitation Under 18
13. NEHC Medal

A schedule of classes

Decoration of tack stalls begins like this . . .

27

. . . and ends like these

Overheard — HSM to HSM (watching a junior rider accept a silver bowl): "To heck with ribbons, let's go for the silver."

Championships

Some shows offer championships and reserve championships in selected divisions. Check the Prize List for rules governing these awards. Quite often the championships are awarded in accordance with the AHSA requirements for hunter championships, with the championship and reserve championship titles given to two of the four ponies with the most points in the over fences phase of the division. In addition to these points, only these four ponies receive half points for ribbons won in model classes and full points for ribbons won in one under saddle class.

For these purposes, five points are given for first place, three points for second, two for third and one for fourth. Now, suppose that the division in question is a large pony hunter division which includes six classes: large pony hunter under saddle, large pony conformation hunter, large pony working hunter, large pony working hunter, large pony working hunter, and large pony model. First a determination is made as to which four ponies have earned the highest number of points in the conformation hunter class and the three working hunter classes. Then, only those four ponies receive points for the model class and the under saddle class. Since only half points are awarded for the model class, a pony taking first in the model class receives two-and-a-half points, with one-and-a-half points given for second place, etc. They receive full points for the under saddle class. The pony receiving the highest number of points is then awarded the championship with the reserve championship going to the pony with the second highest number of points.

If there is a tie score, the award is given to the pony with the highest number of points over fences. If the tie is still unbroken, the contending ponies may be called back into the ring for a ride-off. If the championship is not governed by AHSA rules, the criteria for this award will be explained in the Prize List.

Mother's Aid

You should be aware that show secretaries can make errors (usually in transcribing) in determining the championship awards. Since the award is merely a function of the points awarded in the division, you might keep track informally of who won the top four ribbons in each class of the division in question. You should also keep a record of the show results of both the pony and the child and submit it to the AHSA for year-end awards; it is too expensive not to keep track. We also found that insurance companies want a list of a pony's shows and results when insuring or raising the insurance of a show pony.

HUNTER SECTIONS

Hunter Courses: The course offered will consist of at least eight jumps with one or two changes of direction. The fences will simulate obstacles found in the hunt field, including brush, post and rail, walls, gates, coops, and in and outs.

Under Saddle Classes: Entries to be shown at a walk, trot, and canter both ways of the ring. Light contact with the horse's mouth is required. Horses should be obedient, alert, and move freely. They should not be eliminated for slight errors. No martingales are permitted. In Regular, Amateur Owner, Junior, and Pony Hunter Sections, entries may be asked to hand gallop collectively one way of the ring, at the judge's discretion. No more than eight entries shall be asked to hand gallop at one time.

Green Hunter: A Green Hunter is a horse of any age in his first or second year of showing at regular member of AHSA or CEF shows in classes with fences 3'6" or higher. Horses may cross enter between the Green Working and the Green Conformation Sections or any other sections wherever eligible. First Year Horses to jump 3'6"; Second Year horses to jump 3'9". The model class will be judged on conformation, way of moving, and soundness. In the Green Conformation Section, performance will be judged at 60% and conformation at 40%

Over Fences Classes: All over fences classes will be judged on performance and soundness. Conformation, if applicable, will be specified with the appropriate classes. Manners will be emphasized in the Adult Hunter, Amateur Owner Hunter, Junior Hunter, and Pony Hunter Sections. Extreme speed will be penalized in the Junior Hunter and Pony Hunter Sections. Suitability of the pony to the rider will be emphasized in the Pony Hunter Section.

Amateur Owner Hunter: To be ridden by Amateur Owner or by an amateur member of the owner's family, as defined under AHSA Rule IX. Fences at 3'6". Horses and riders may cross enter into the Adult Amateur Hunter Section.

Adult Amateur Hunter: To be ridden by an Amateur as defined under AHSA Rules. Fences at 3'0" in height.

Pony Hunter: Open to ponies ridden by a junior exhibitor. All ponies must have a current measurement card issued by the AHSA. A Small Pony does not exceed 12.2 hands; a Medium Pony is larger than 12.2 hands but does not exceed 13.2 hands; and a Large Pony is larger than 13.2 hands but does not exceed 14.2 hands. Model Class will be judged on conformation, soundness, and way of moving. The under saddle class will be judged 25% on Conformation.

Children's Hunter: Open to horses and ponies to be ridden by any junior exhibitor under 15 years of age. Junior exhibitors 15-17 years must be eligible for limit equitation over fences as of December 1st of the current show year. Fences to be set from 2'6" to 3'0" in height. Horses and ponies to show over the same course and the same height. Neither rider nor mount may cross enter into any rated hunter or jumper class over fences, with the exception of horsemanship. Classes to be judged on performance and soundness with emphasis on manners. Extreme speed will be penalized.

Low Hunter: Open to horses and ponies of any age regardless of prior winnings and qualifications. Fences at 3'0"

Schooling Hunter: Open to horses and ponies. Fences to be set at 2'6" to 2'9". If sufficient pony entries warrant, class will be split and run as two separate classes. Ponies must be ridden by a junior. Ponies will be judged at 2'6" only if class is split.

JUMPER SECTIONS

Ties: All ties involving first place will be jumped off as specified. In all other ties, prize money will be divided equally and riders will toss a coin for ribbons unless otherwise specified.

Training Jumpers: Open to all horses regardless of prior winnings. Fences will be from 3'3" to 3'9" in height, with spreads from 3' to 4'.

Junior/Amateur Owner Jumpers: All horses must be recorded with the AHSA. Horses must be ridden by Amateur Owners or by an amateur member of the owner's family. Jumps will be 3'6" to 4'6" in height with spreads from 4' to 5'.

A description of classes

30

Schedule

Overheard — HSM to HSM: "On Sundays I go home from the show. On Monday and Tuesday I do all the laundry from it. On Wednesday I get ready to leave for the next one which starts on Thursday . . . and suddenly I find myself back at Sunday."

The Prize List contains a schedule of the classes. For this reason alone you should always retain possession of a copy. If someone needs to take a quick look at it, be sure you get it back. Be aware that this schedule can be altered; the order of classes can be revised (notification of this is usually made over the P.A. system). A class can be cancelled if there are not enough entries and it can be moved to a ring other than the one specified in the Prize List. We learned this the hard way; one of the authors arrived *on time* for her daughter's model class at the Pony Finals only to discover that the class had been held an hour earlier.

Overheard — HSM to HSM: "Is this Friday or Saturday? Let's see . . . what class are we on?"

Stabling for Ponies and Other Less Important Mammals
Or: If You Don't Hurry, There's "No Room at the Inn."

The Prize List often provides information about housing for both yourself and the pony. If stabling is available you need to know the following:

What is the charge?

What arrangements need to be made to ensure that several ponies are stabled together?

Must the pony be stabled in the show's facilities?

Under what circumstances are stall fees refunded?

Are tack stalls available?

Do you need to provide a stall guard? A stall guard is a webbing of heavy material (often canvas) which attaches to both sides of the door to the stall with hooks and eyes and acts as a barrier to equine-escape. We were at somewhat of a disadvantage when we arrived at our first "away" show with ponies in hand, only to discover that not all stalls come with doors.

Is bedding provided? Bedding is a soft, absorbent, inexpensive material which is spread over the stall floor. Find out what kind of bedding is provided; some ponies are allergic to certain types of bedding.

Still more requirements . . .

When are the stalls available and when must they be vacated?

Be aware that buckets for water and feed are not provided by the management.

Mother's Aid
Bring hooks and eyes to hang the buckets in the stalls.

Can you buy hay, grain, and bedding at all times at the show? It is no fun to arrive at the show grounds at 9 PM only to find that bedding and feed are not available until noon the next day.

You should know that standing stalls are narrow, usually with three walls. Ponies in standing stalls are tied up and not free to move around. Box stalls are larger enclosures with four walls; ponies are not tied up in box stalls and therefore can move around. Tack stalls are rooms in which tack can be stored. You need to bring racks for saddles, hooks for hanging bridles, and tack boxes for storing other equipment. Tack stalls have also been known to house humans . . . and can be candidates for *House and Garden* decorating awards.

The Prize List may include general information about hotels near the showgrounds. If you want more specific recommendations contact the show secretary.

Warning — The show secretary may recommend a particular hotel as good because "that's where they always put up the judges." If at all possible, select other accommodations. The chances are very good that you will either: (a) want to celebrate, or b) want to drown your sorrows. Under neither circumstance do you want to be sharing the dining room or lounge with the judge of the show.

Short tail — One HSM recently found her enormous van parked in next to a spiffy, little BMW at 6:30 AM. While she cursed, she maneuvered the van up and down a steep embankment. She got out and checked the proximity of the spare tire on the van to the passenger door of the car. Starting to climb back in the driver's seat she heard a cheerful but anxious shout from the first floor balcony, "Let me help you!" The voice and the BMW belonged to the judge. She is only grateful that her daughter's pony doesn't resemble the van.

There are several other considerations to bear in mind. Try to secure a room in a hotel that is as close as possible to the showgrounds. Five or ten minutes difference in driving time may seem negligible when you make the reservations; but we can ssure you that your perspective will change when you have to run a few kids to the showgrounds at five in the morning so that they can braid, or one of your competitors forgets an important piece of personal tack such as her jacket.

Mother's Aid

Make your reservations for stalls and hotel rooms early. Many shows are popular and if you delay, you may find there is "no room at the inn."

There is much more to a hotel than bed, bath, and color television. For instance, restaurant facilities permit the adults to dine at their leisure when the children need to be in bed early. Swimming pools seem to help children make the transition from competitors to friends. If noncompeting siblings are along, a pool helps them feel as if they are on vacation.

Mother's Aid

Unless your competitor has an extensive wardrobe of show clothes, it is helpful if laundry facilities are on the premises. We found that while jodphurs are often beige, mud is always dark brown.

Classes

The Prize List of a show describes all of the classes. You must read the fine print to determine the eligibility requirements for each class: the restrictions can apply to the pony, the rider, or both. For instance, equitation classes can be divided according to age and the ability of the rider. The latter is determined by the number of blue ribbons won in equitation classes:

Maiden classes are limited to riders who have not won a blue ribbon.

Novice classes are limited to riders who have not won three blue ribbons.

Limit classes are open to riders who have not won six blue ribbons.

Open classes are open to all riders.

In hunter seat equitations blue ribbons won on the flat do not affect the rider's status for equitation classes over fences. However, blue ribbons won over fences do affect the rider's status for equitation classes on the flat.

Sometimes the restrictions apply to the animal. An example of this would be classes open only to ponies. 14.2 hands separates ponies from horses (and nothing else); anything over 14.2 hands is a horse. Sometimes the class is restricted to certain registered breeds.

The restrictions can also apply to both rider and mount. For instance, most shows restrict their pony classes to junior exhibitors. Junior exhibitors are those riders who have not reached their eighteenth birthday by the beginning of the show year (which for AHSA purposes is currently December 1).

Overheard — HSM to HSM: "I don't know why they call *this* class special."

34

A quiet moment

American Horse Shows Association, Inc.
The National Equestrian Federation of the United States
220 East 42nd Street, New York, NY 10017-5806
(212) 972-AHSA

OFFICIAL MEASUREMENT FORM
Valid for 45 days after date indicated below

NO FEE FOR AHSA MEMBERS • $10.00 FEE FOR NON-MEMBERS

ONCE FORM HAS BEEN SURRENDERED TO THE AHSA OFFICE, NO ADDITIONS, CHANGES AND/OR
DELETIONS CAN BE MADE. ALL QUESTIONS MUST BE ANSWERED.

ANIMAL'S NAME _____ AHSA RECORDING # _____

COLOR _____ SEX _____ YEAR FOALED _____

MARKINGS (Absence of markings must be indicated) _____

HEAD: _____

BODY: _____

LEGS: _____

OWNER: _____ ____ MEMBER, AHSA # _____

ADDRESS: _____ ____ NON-MEMBER*

_____

_____
(Signature of person providing information)
Must be 18 years of age or older

FORM MUST BE SIGNED BY THE PERSON FURNISHING THE ABOVE INFORMATION IMMEDIATELY
BEFORE THE ANIMAL IS MEASURED.

Animal must be measured and form must be signed by any two of the three officials acting together: a veterinarian, a
Judge or a Steward who is officiating in the show at which the animal is measured.

_____ 19_____

We hereby certify that we measured this animal at the _____ Horse Show.

Its height is _____ hands _____ inches and is SHOD _____ UNSHOD _____
                                                                    Height of heel from
SHOD ONLY IN FRONT _____ SHOD ONLY BEHIND _____   coronet to ground

_____   _____
Veterinarian/Judge/Steward   Veterinarian/Judge/Steward

*I hereby certify that I have received $10.00 for the measurement of the above animal.

_____
(Steward)

PINK—AHSA COPY • WHITE—OWNER'S COPY

AHSA Official Measurement Form

Coggins Test Form

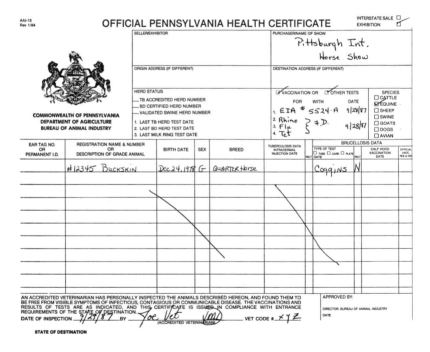

A sample Health Certificate

Judging Specifications

The Prize List includes information about how the classes are to be judged. This may necessitate consulting the AHSA Rule Book since many Prize Lists simply state that a particular class is to be judged in accordance with AHSA Rules. The class description also specifies whether it is to be held on the flat or over fences. The maximum height of the fences will be designated for the over fences classes.

Miscellaneous Information

You should always check the Prize List for additional rules, regulations, and information. For instance, it should advise you whether dogs are permitted on the showgrounds. It may provide information about what types of tack room decorations are allowed. Special facilities for camper parking may be available (and rservations may be mandatory). Some shows restrict the use of golf carts. Some HSMs also restrict the use of golf carts.

Often overheard — Child to HSM: "But Mother, why can't you ask about renting a golf cart?"

The Prize List should have information about schooling — when riders are permitted to school their ponies, where schooling is permitted, and whether an additional fee is charged for use of the schooling ring. It is not much fun to arrive at an *A* show to find that the only schooling was held two days earlier.

Last, but not least, check the Prize List to see whether an exhibitor's party is planned.

Paperwork (Red Tape)

The Prize List will specify what credentials or certificates you must bring to the show. These might include:

1) *Pony Measurement Card* — This card states the official measurement of the animal along with the shoeing status of the pony at the time of measurement and the height of the heel (the animal must be shown the same way that it was when measured). If the animal is under six years of age, it must be remeasured yearly; once the animal is six years old, it is issued a permanent card.

If you do not have a measurement card, the animal can be measured when competing at a recognized show for a fee of $10 for non-AHSA members (measurements for members are free). When you arrive at the show, tell the secretary that you have a pony that needs to be measured. Two officials (veterinarian, judge or steward) measure the animal. You have to fill out the form, so take a pen when you take the pony.

Do not leave any blanks on the form. If the pony does not have an AHSA number, write *not recorded* (or something to that effect); if there are no markings, you must indicate the absence.

The official completes the form after measuring the animal. He must indicate the date of the measurement, name of the horse show, height of the animal, shoeing status (shod or unshod), and height of the heel from the coronet to the ground. Then both officials must sign the form. If a fee has been received for the measurement, this must be indicated on the form. Again, the form must be filled out completely for the measurement to count.

Mother's Aid
Don't take any chances; check the form yourself for completeness and accuracy.

If you own a pony that is borderline for the height division in which you wish to show it, have a professional take it to be measured. Not only is a pony's height affected by its weight and shoeing status, but also by the way that it is stood up for the measurement.

After the animal has been measured and the form completed, the white copy is returned to the owner and the pink is sent to the AHSA. Since it will be a few weeks before the measurement card is sent to the owner, the white copy is valid for 45 days from the date that the animal was measured.

2. *Coggins Test* — A negative test for Equine Infectious Anemia is required at most shows. A veterinarian must draw a blood specimen to test for it.

Mother's Aid
Since the blood is usually sent away to a lab, allow several weeks for the results (do not ask your vet for a coggins test two days before the competition).

3) *Health Papers* — There are health certificates, signed by a veterinarian, attesting to the good health of the animal; these are usually valid for a limited time period. The forms vary from state to state. The veterinarian examines the animal for contagious diseases. He will need to know whether the animal's vaccinations are up-to-date, the name and address of the owner, the destination of the animal, and a complete description of the animal (for the Coggins test). If the owner is traveling separately from the animal, the health papers should be carried by the person driving the horse trailer. Then, if the need arises, the driver can demonstrate to any official's satisfaction that the animal is healthy. This is a requirement when you travel across state lines.

4) *AHSA membership cards (for the exhibitors)* — This card proves eligibility to participate in classes at shows which are restricted to AHSA members. It is also required to waive fees for measurements and for

FEB.   APPLICATION FOR HORSE RECORDING   No. _____

1. Name of Horse _____

2. Previous name of horse and/or owner _____

3. Division(s) shown in _____

4. Color _____ 5. Sex _____ 6. Height _____ 7. Year Foaled _____

8. Sire _____ 9. Dam _____

10. Markings _____

_____

11. Breed_____

12. Breed Registry Name & Number _____

13. Owner(s) (Name as entered in horse show)* _____

_____ AHSA No. _____

14. Address _____ Tel. No. _____

Recording Fee for the life of the horse; $75.
IMPORTANT: *Affiliate Members are not eligible for Horse of the Year Awards or other trophies.

*Entries may be made in a Farm, Corporation, etc., name for Horse of the Year Awards provided such name is registered with AHSA ($75) and one AHSA recorded owner must be a Senior, Junior or Life member.

Points will not count until the application and fees for the horse's recording, exhibitor registration, transfer of ownership, name change or addition of owner(s) and owner's Senior, Junior or Life membership are received by the AHSA office; It is further provided that for points to count with respect to any competition, such materials and fees must be received by the AHSA office on or before the first recognized day of such competition.

The AHSA will not be held responsible for late, delayed, or misdirected mail.

Please refer to current edition of AHSA Rule Book for further eligibility requirements.

_____
Signature   I hereby certify that I am the owner/agent of the above animal.

A sample of an Application for Horse Recording form

THE AMERICAN HORSE SHOWS ASSOCIATION, INC.
220 East 42nd Street
New York, N.Y. 10017-5806
212/972-AHSA

Enclosed is my payment of $ _____ for membership in the AHSA for the
year _____ (Membership expires November 30.)

LIFE . . . . $750   JUNIOR (must give birthdate ____/____/____) . . . $35
SENIOR . . . . $50   AFFILIATE (must give name of Association with which
                                  affiliated) _____ . . . $20

NAME _____
        Title   First Name   Middle Initial   Last Name

ADDRESS _____

_____
City   State   Zip Code

TELEPHONE _____
        Day #   Phone #

AMATEUR APPLICATION

I certify that I have read and understand the Amateur Rule as published in the most current edition of the AHSA Rule Book and am eligible for amateur status under all conditions of the rule. AMATEUR STATUS MUST BE RENEWED ANNUALLY. (Junior Exhibitors are exempt and cannot apply).

Age Group (Check one)   18-30 years (   )   Over 30 years (   )

Signature of applicant above: _____
                    application for amateur status will not be processed without signature.

A sample application for membership in the AHSA

39

participation in AHSA-recognized shows. If you are not a member, every Prize List of an AHSA-recognized show includes an application for membership. To join, you merely compete the form and return it to the AHSA with your dues.

Mother's Aid
The dues for junior membership are minimal when you consider what you get in return. A member can have her pony measured for no charge. Members do not have to pay special fees to compete in AHSA-recognized shows. A member receives a copy of the current rule book and issues of *Horse Show* magazine which publishes a calendar of show dates and lists revisions of rules, among other things. Also, a pony can only be registered with the AHSA if it is owned by an AHSA member.

5) *AHSA recording numbers (for the animals)* — An animal must be recorded with the AHSA in order for points, won at recognized shows, to be counted; points can only be accumulated if the animal is registered with the AHSA. In addition, in order to compete in the Pony Finals, a pony must be recorded with the AHSA prior to the date of the show in which it qualified.

Mother's Aid
Since the results of a show will not count unless the application and fees have been received by the AHSA prior to the date of the show, send the form and fees in well before the show date. It is difficult to explain to a ten-year-old child that, although she won a Championship in the pony hunter division, the pony can't go to the pony finals because you haven't recorded the pony with the AHSA.

Mother's Aid
You need to know your pony's color, markings, age, and sex in order to complete entry forms, insurance forms, applications for measurement cards, and AHSA registration. If you are new to the equine world, you may be surprised to discover that, for instance, brown ponies are not *brown* and white ponies are not *white*. Here is a summary of those bits of equine trivia needed to complete the paperwork for showing. Knowing colors helps in following performance where ponies are often differentiated in discussion by color or markings, as in: "That bay with the blaze moves well."

Colors of Ponies

Bay — A brown pony with dark points (points: mane, tail and leg trim).
Chestnut (sorrell) — A brown pony without black points.
Palomino — A golden brown with white points.
Buckskin — A golden brown with black points.

Gray — A white pony with hints of dark points (the only white ponies called white are those with pink or blue eyes, which may also be called albinos); grays are usually a dark color at birth and lighten as they age.

Roan — A solid color pony with white hairs mixed into the coat uniformly; a black and white mix is a blue roan and a brown and white mix is a strawberry roan.

Pintos/paints/appaloosas — Spotted ponies.

Green (a horse of a different color) — According to the AHSA, ponies are green if they have not been shown over fences at the regulation height or higher for their respective section at a Regular Member show of the AHSA (or the Canadian Equestrian Federation) prior to December 1st of the previous year. According to our five-year-old, a green pony is one he has never seen.

Markings of Ponies

Star — A small white spot on the forehead.

Snip — A white mark on the lower part of the nose.

Blaze A white stripe running down the pony's face (sometimes symmetrical, often not).

Bald face — A white mark so wide it covers the pony's eyes and face.

Socks — White markings below the pastern.

Stockings — White markings which go up the knees.

Sex and Age

There are three genders (easier to differentiate in ponies than in most foreign languages):

Stallions — Male ponies that have not been castrated.

Mares — Female ponies.

Geldings — Castrated male ponies.

Mother's Aid

One of the authors had to be corrected by her child when, in filling out a form, she indicated the sex of a gelding pony as *M*. Geldings are designated by *G*, mares by *M*, and stallions by *S*.

Other Linguistic Idiosyncrasies — A young male is called a colt, a young female a filly, and all ponies under one year are foals.

Age — Although we won't go into figuring age by teeth, we are told that this is possible (ask your local expert). For showing purposes the ages of ponies are calculated from January 1 of the year. *Note:* the ages of exhibitors are calculated from December 1 of the year; this coincides with the AHSA calendar.

CC

Markings of ponies

MAIL ALL ENTRIES & PAYMENTS TO:

Elmira Charity Horse Show
R.D.2, 4562 Middle Road
Horseheads, N.Y. 14845
(607) 739-7375 or 739-4443

ELMIRA CHARITY HORSE SHOW
JULY 9 - 12, 1987
ENTRY BLANK
ONLY ONE HORSE PER BLANK

ENTRY NO.

Complete ALL OWNER INFORMATION

Name _____

Address _____

_____

Phone _____

Rider Address (Equitation)

_____

NAME OF HORSE					NAME OF RIDER				
	HUNTER								RIDER AHSA #
	CLASSES								
	JUMPER								
HORSE AHSA #	SEX	AGE		COLOR	HEIGHT		1st GREEN	2nd GREEN	
	EQUITATION CLASSES								
RIDER				USET NO.	AGE OF JR./AM	ASPCA No.		AHSA No.	

$10 Schooling Fee _____

$8.00 Non-Member Fee _____

$4.00 AHSA Drug Fee _____

$40.00 Camper _____

$60.00 Box Stalls _____

Total Entry Fees _____

Total Fees _____

"Every entry at a recognized show shall constitute an agreement and affirmation that the person making it, along with the owner, lessee, trainer, manager, agent, coach, driver, rider, and the horse: (1) shall be subject to the constitution and rules of the association and the local rules of the show; (2) that every horse, rider, and/or driver is eligible as enters; (3) that the owner and any of his representatives are bound by the constitution and rules of the AHSA and the show and will accept as final the decision of the hearing committee on any question arising under said rules and agree to hold the show, the AHSA, their officials, director and employees harmless for any action taken; (4) that the owner, rider/driver and any of their agents or representatives agree to hold the AHSA, the show, and their officials, directors, employees and age its harmless for any injury or loss suffered during or in connection with the show, whether or not such injury or loss esulted, directly or indirectly, from the negligent acts or omissions of said officials, directors, employees or agents of the AHSA or show. The construction or application of AHSA rules is governed by the State of New York".

Entry and stall fees must accompany this form. For VISA/Master Charge, see blank in prize list.

OWNER/AGENT SIGNATURE _____ AHSA No. _____

TRAINER'S SIGNATURE _____ AHSA No. _____

ADDRESS _____

STABLE WITH _____ PHONE _____

Coggins _____

Meas. Card _____

AHSA Amat. _____

Number of Stall Gates Needed _____

A sample Entry Blank

2

Between Martinet
and Martini

Martinet — According to Webster's, a martinet is a
very strict disciplinarian or stickler for rigid
regulations. According to the horse show child, this
describes the HSM. This is how you may not be
seen by the trainer who sometimes wishes you were
more of a martinet. *Martini* — According to
Webster's, a mixture of gin and vermouth;
according to Cole Porter, the fountain of youth;
and according to us on some show nights, the only
alternative.

T HE HSM HAS THE PRIZE LIST and has returned the
completed entry form to the show secretary. Now she's ready to go to the
show. But first . . . she has to pack. She has to pack for the pony. She has to
pack for the child. And she has to pack for herself.

Here is the HSM guide to equipment for the pony, i.e. those things your
child might demand you purchase, fetch, fasten, tighten or take off:

Halter — This is the basic piece of tack the pony uses when it is not
being ridden. The halter is the easiest piece of tack to put on once you get
the hang of it. Slip it up over the nose with the other strap going behind the
ears, then clip or buckle it.

Lead shank — A lead shank is a rope of nylon, cloth or leather with
which you (or with luck someone else) lead the pony. It has a clip at one end
which fastens to a metal circle on the bottom strap of the halter (under the
pony's chin). It may also have a chain, just before the clip, which can be

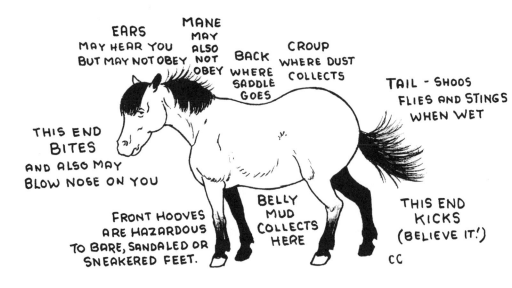

HSM PONY PARTS to REMEMBER

Leave room for the yum-yums!

44

fastened over the pony's nose for more control when leading it. A lead shank is also called a leadrope.

Bridle — You are allowed to bridle* a bit if asked to put this one on. It is the headgear of the pony when someone is riding it. The bridle has a number of straps: headpiece, checkstrap, noseband (cavesson), browband, throat latch, bit, reins (all of which have to be fastened). You carry it (as in, "Quick, Mom, get my bridle!") by slipping the top strap, called the headpiece, over your shoulder and then looping the reins over your shoulder too, so that the bridle hangs from your shouldr the way it is going to hang on the pony (bridles can get very tangled). *Special bridling tip*: Take a moment to look carefully at a bridle before the first show.

Bit — The metal part of a bridle inserted in the pony's mouth. There are literally hundreds of bits; for the HSM it is enough to know two: 1) The *snaffle* is a jointed metal bit with two large rings to which single reins are attached. Into this category fall the most commonly used snaffles, as in, "Would you give me the *full cheek*?", which has nothing to do with turning the other cheek; or, "I need an *eggbutt*", which has nothing to do with breakfast or one's posterior; or, "Where's my *D ring*?", which has nothing to do with the finger unless, of course, you can't find it; or, "I need the *edge*.', which has nothing to do with the fact that we all need an edge at horse shows. *Warning: small bits can be hard to find at tack stores.* 2) The *pelham* bit has a chain that goes under the pony's chin. This bit is like the snaffle in that it acts on the corners of the mouth; it is controlled by one set of reins. A second set of reins controls the chain which brings the pony's head in toward its chest.

Mother's Aid
The most efficient means of cleaning bits that we know is to put them in the dishwasher (if they're really dirty, first scrub them with steel wool). Just remember to take them out for the show.

We know one rider who brought all of her bits home to clean the night before a show. In the morning she took out only those she planned to use at the show. The HSM came down at 8 AM, panicked when she saw bits in the dishwasher, jumped in the car, and raced to the show grounds. Seeing her daughter on the schooling field, she drove across the field and jumped out of the car, waving the bits in the air and yelling her daughter's name. This HSM was dressed in pink fuzzy slippers, bathrobe, and curlers.

Martingale — When we looked up the definition, we found that it fell most appropriately between martinet and martini. It is a strap or straps, one of which attaches at one end to the girth (which is slipped through the larger loop in the martingale) and at the other end to the noseband of the

---

*Bridle — To show hostility or resentment especially by drawing back the head and chin.

45

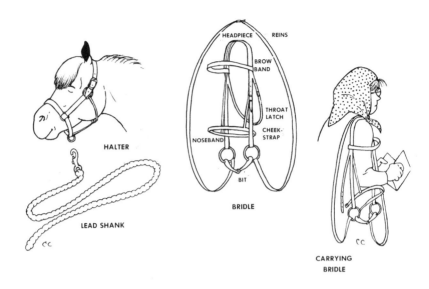

HEADPIECE   REINS

BROW
BAND

THROAT
LATCH

CHEEK-
STRAP

NOSEBAND

BIT

HALTER

BRIDLE

LEAD SHANK

CARRYING
BRIDLE

A halter, lead shank, bridle and HSM carrying the bridle properly

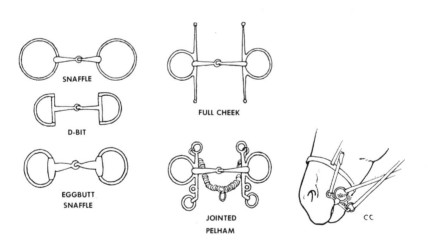

SNAFFLE

FULL CHEEK

D-BIT

EGGBUTT
SNAFFLE

JOINTED
PELHAM

Bits

46

bridle (standing martingale); or the strap separates and has two loops, through which the reins are threaded and then re-buckled (running martingale). The other strap encircles the pony's neck and meets the first on the pony's chest. A martingale has a buckle and holes in the loop which fits around the girth and thus may be shortened . . . as in, "Mrs. Doe, Jenny's martingale is too long." The *doughnut* is a little rubber circle threaded onto the martingale to keep the straps from slipping where they cross; it is also the breakfast of choice for young riders. *Note:* martingales are only worn in classes with an over fence phase. They are, however, often worn when the child and pony are in training, in order to help the pony carry itself in a more correct frame.

Reins — A line fastened to a bit on each side by which a rider controls an animal (we hope). Reins may be made of leather, webb, or rubber (nonslip); usually they are joined by a single hole buckle at the very end of each strap. The term *riding on the buckle* means that the reins are held at the buckle; they will then be long and loose.

Saddle — A . . . usually padded and leather-covered seat for a rider on horseback. From the HSM's point of view this is the heaviest, most expensive part of a child's tack; and though there are many different kinds, styles and sizes (children outgrow them just as they outgrow breeches and boots), saddles still tend to look pretty much the same when sharing a rack in the tack room. One solution is to attach a nameplate on the cantle of the saddle. (It's bad enough to have to carry a saddle and position it on the pony's back correctly; it's worse if the saddle is someone else's and you have to start over.)

Saddles have lots of parts; here are some that you might have to use when helping your child:

Girth — As in, "Mom, could you tighten my girth?" (which often needs doing after pony has begun working). It is a leather or webbing belt which encircles the belly of a horse to fasten on the saddle. A girth has two buckles at each end; the buckles are often attached to elastic straps at the end which is fastened on the left side of the pony.

Saddle pad — As in, "Mom, my saddle pad is slipping." It is the pad that goes on the horse's back, under the saddle. Although it has the capability of lying flat and extending evenly around the saddle, it rarely does so without encouragement. There are many varieties in many colors. You will find, however, that pads used for showing are always white. We feel, therefore, that the most important things for the HSM to know about a saddle pad are how to wash it and that she did. Most saddle pads attach to the saddle in some way, usually with a webbing lop which fits around the straps to which you attach the girth. In theory this prevents slippage.

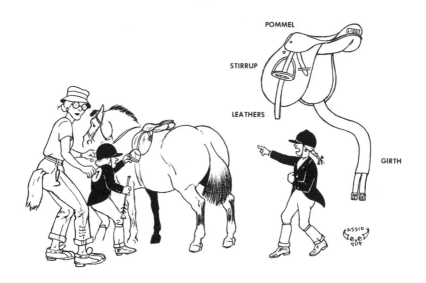

" . . . mine!"

"Crop or bat - used by child on pony to wake him up."

Stirrups — As in, "Mom, run up my stirrups please," or, "Mom, my stirrups need shortening." A stirrup is a "ring made horizontal in one part for receiving the foot of a rider, attached by a strap to a saddle, and used to aid in mounting and as a support while riding." (Webster's)

Stirrup cup — A farewell drink which the situation may demand once your child is mounted and off to the class; you should feel entitled to enjoy a cup of your favorite beverage either for courage, for your patience and perseverance or, of course, purely for hydration.

Leathers — These are leather, belt-like straps on which the stirrups hang. Leathers are fastened to the saddle by being slipped onto a little metal bar up under the skirt of the saddle. This bar always remains flat and open so that both leather and stirrup come off the saddle if your child comes off the pony. Actually, these leathers are what need shortening or lengthening, as in, "Mom, my stirrups need shortening." This is done easily by pulling the buckle down from the metal bar where it normally rests, undoing the buckle, and letting it down a hole or taking it up one. Your child, by now used to being helped (leathers can be shortened or lengthened by a mounted child), will accommodatingly move her leg forward and out of the way.

Crouper — The croup is defined by Webster's as "the rump of a quadruped." The crouper is a strap which goes along the center of the rump of a specific quadruped, the horse. At one end it is attached to the back of the saddle and at the other end it has a loop which goes around the tail of the pony. The crouper keeps the saddle from sliding too far forward.

Mother's Aid
The crouper is best left attached to the saddle. With the inordinate number of straps involved in tack, it is best to simplify where you can in order to avoid misplacing and losing things.

Crop (bat) — A riding whip with a short, straight stock and a loop. It is used by a child on a pony to wake it up. The temptation to be avoided here for use on the child by the mother, as in, "Straighten her up!"

Spurs — A spur is a pointed device worn on the heel of the riding boot and is used to prick the pony's side, to urge it forward.

Leg wraps — These are long strips of flannel, cotton, or synthetic knit which are wrapped around the pony's legs, over quilts when shipping, around medication or ice packs, and as protection when schooling, riding cross-country, or providing support after a workout. Leg wraps are the equestrian version of supphose.

Quilts — These are rectangular quilted cotton pads which are wrapped around the pony's legs for protection.

Two Sheets to the Wind (Or Other Necessities)

Sheet — A broad piece of cloth, usually cotton on canvas. It is used to keep the pony clean and warm at the show, discourage hair growth as days and nights get cooler, and keep the chills away when shipping. Sheets come in all sizes (except the special-ordered-pony-small that hasn't come in yet) — and colors, except the color of manure and the right color to match the pony with the taste of the child and the HSM.

Mother's Aid
Plaids don't seem to look as dirty.

Double sheeting — Two sheets to the wind. When it's getting colder, but not cold enough for a blanket, you can put two (or more) sheets on the pony. The challenge is to buckle the sheet tightly enough so that it doesn't slip.

Mother's Aid
Memorize the phone number of the weather service; this will help ou in answering your child's query whether the pony needs one sheet or none, two sheets or one, or a blanket . . . especially when the child wants to return to the barn to add or subtract a layer.

Short tail — One of our ponies recently was found early in the morning standing over its still-attached, urine-soaked, very ripped sheet which had just been mended. Yes, it can be repaired . . . and repaired . . . and repaired. And yes, we now buy second-hand sheets.

Fly sheet — Another version of the broad piece of cloth, this one is made of netting to keep off the flies. This is especially helpful at ringside on a pony with a mud tail who cannot use it to flick away flies.

Rain sheet — Picture your well-groomed child astride her glossy pony in her costly clothes, boots, and velvet hat; picture her sitting on her expensive leather saddle; and picture a downpour. Now picture a canvas sheet to drape over them. That is a rain sheet.

Mother's Aid
Shower curtains have been known to double as rain sheets; you can also try the thicker plastic drop sheets used by painters.

Cooler — Most coolers look like regular blankets. They are wool or acrylic blend rectangles with a forehead strap and a tail strap and two ties for the chest. They are used after a workout to absorb sweat and keep the pony from getting a chill. Fancier coolers are fitted over the rump, buckle in the front, and have a hidden surcingle which goes under the belly. Webster's has three definitions of a cooler: "one that cools." — obviously the above; "an iced drink with an alcohoic beverage as base." — obviously

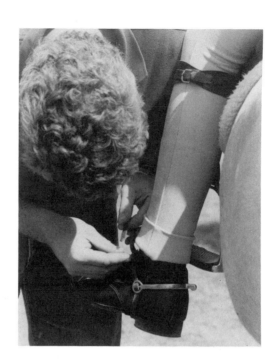

Fastening on spurs

Travelling wraps secured
with masking tape

51

"Mommy, think you've got the back strap too tight."

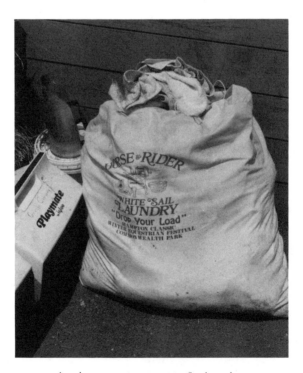

A unique way to separate the laundry

Child and pony in rain gear

Where is their rain gear now?

the kind that a harried HSM might need; and "a cell for violent prisoners." — a consideration for the obstreperous show child.

A cooler is also used after a warm-up and before a class. It can be wrapped around several shivering children at a time, or a chilled HSM (and is then more appropriately called a *warm(h)er*.

Blanket — A large, usually oblong piece of woven fabric used as a body covering. It comes in different sizes, colors, styles, and weights. It is used to keep the pony warm while in the stall and prevent a heavy winter coat coming in and turning a show pony into a shaggy pony. Some blankets have matching hoods to keep the coat thin on its face and neck as well. The complete outfit, blanket and hood, looks a bit like medieval armor when the pony is suited up. Blankets, like sheets, are cut to fit the body and fasten on one side with straps which go under yhe belly and buckle on the other side. Sometimes these straps cross, sometimes they don't. Some blankets go over the head while others fasten at the chest. Some ponies are difficult about having something put over their heads, just like human babies. For them a blanket that slips over the back and fastens at the chest is easier.

Mother's Aid
Purchase a good quality blanket. It will save you money in the end because it will last longer and wear better. Never purchase a blanket-and-hood combination without first getting directions on how to assemble the outfit. The first cold day this year found two bewildered HSMs fumbling with no less than eight different straps, four snaps, and many holes in which various parts of the pony's anatomy were supposed to poke through. The pony was more patient than the mothers and, in the end, was blanketed sans hood. Blankets and sheets and coolers may be washable but either: 1) use public washers for large items (line dry to avoid shrinkage); or 2) if you wash at home don't combine a load of horse stuff with your husband's underwear. We did. Remember how scratchy horsehair chairs were in the olden days? Well . . .

Challenge — When you disrobe the pony be careful where you put the clothing; neighboring horses often regard these items as edible, or at least shredable.

Mother's Aid
A blanket can rub hair off the pony, leaving ugly bald spots. This sometimes occurs if the blanket doesn't fit properly. You can remove the blanket, try to make it fit better, or sew a silky-smooth lining where rubbing occurs.

Pony Pacifier — And finally, here is the one piece of equipment for the pony which is not available in a tack store or mail order catalog. We know that someone is going to make a fortune designing a pacifier for ponies that

54

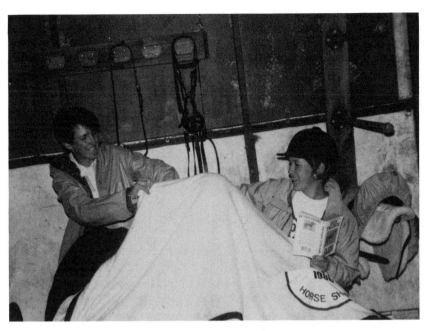

Warming up with a cooler

Ready to go into the ring

exhibit teething behavior (the urge to chew, nibble, and drool) long after their teeth are in.

Mother's Aid
The HSM pacifier could be a "thank you" from child or trainer, a call from the Horse Show Father, or someone handing her a cold drink.

Equipment for the Child

Let's take it from the top. Here is what the best dressed riders will wear (Remember, you can dress them perfectly even if you can't make them ride perfectly.) and what the HSM needs to pack:

Hard hat — The hat must be an AHSA-approved helmet with a soft peak and a harness which can either be transparent plastic or leather. It also must be velvet, not velveteen. The old Rogers & Hammerstein line of skim milk masquerading as cream won't do.

Short tail — We were caught at the Pony Nationals with velveteen. How gauche! Velvet? Velveteen? You can see the difference when your child is the only one in her division wearing a velveteen helmet.

Shirt — Shirts come in patterns and colors. They come long-sleeve, short sleeve, no sleeve. Girls' shirts have attached choker collars or detachable chokers. The former doesn't get lost, but it tends to look a little less neat. Boys have regular pointed collars.

Mother's Aid
When you think you've lost the choker collar, it is often in the pocket of the jacket. If you buy shirts with detachable chokers, restrict your purchases to shirts of the same color; then when you lose a choker (and you cannot purchase a choker without the shirt), you can substitute one of your other chokers.

Stock pin — They come in all shapes, sizes and price ranges, and are pinned to the center of the choker (boys wear ties with their shirts). We suggest an inexpensive design because this is another small item which, like the choker, tends to get lost. It also tends to get crooked and someone will always point this out, as in, "Mrs. Flanagan, Brigid's stock pin is crooked." Sometimes it helps if another HSM or someone whose fingers aren't numb with nervousness fastens the stock pin.

Breeches — They can be divided into two kinds: regular ones which are worn with high boots and jodhpurs which fit to the ankle and are worn with short boots. Breeches are designed to make riding comfortable and hence are stretchy to accommodate sitting and moving. They fit snugly from the knee down so that there is no bunching, rubbing, or pinching from the movement of the leg against the stirrup leathers and saddle. Dark

56

Ready for schooling or warm-up

Horse Show Child attire for loading the trailer

57

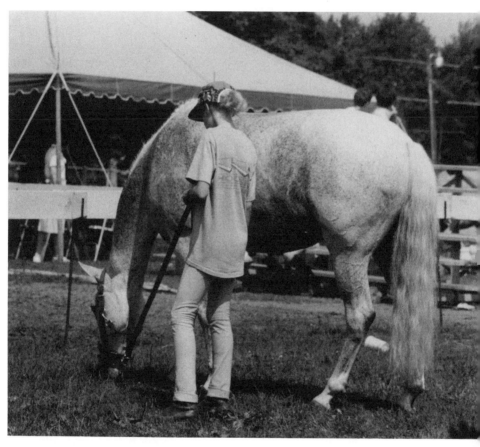

Horse Show Child attire for rewarding the pony at the end of the show day.

colored breeches may look more attractive than tan on heavy riders. And while the heavier weight breeches tend to be more expensive, they often look better on not-so-slim riders. Tan breeches show dirt; rust do not.

Mother's Aid

It is worth trying different brands and sizes to get a good fit since sometimes, even with stretch, there is bagging or the proportions aren't compatible with the body in question, i.e. the leg length is perfect but the waist is too large. Be patient with your child; trying on breeches is much like trying on bathing suits and can be just as discouraging.

Jodhpurs — We agree with Dorothy Henderson Pinch about jods. Here is what she says in *Happy Horsemanship* (Arco) page 118:

Jodhpur breeches, which go all the way down to the ankle, and which are worn with a short jodhpur boot, are the most practical breeches for must riding use, especially for beginners and young, still-growing riders. The cloth over the calf permits a delicate feeling between the rider's leg and the pony's side which is hard to obtain in a high leather boot unless the boot fits perfectly, having been made to your particular measure out of fine soft skins. (Such a boot is naturally quite costly, and it would be foolish to purchase a new pair every six months or so as your feet grow larger and your legs longer.)

Jodhpur boots — Pinch also recommends jodhpur boots for beginners and young riders. She says (p. 118):

Jodhpur boots provide the necessary solid sole and deep heel for proper placement and support on the stirrup iron, and have enough height to protect the ankle from any chafing by the top of the iron. These come ready-made in inexpensive styles, so there is no great losss when they are outgrown and must be replaced. The cheaper high boots are made out of the coarse parts of the cowhide. They make a stiff, unyielding shell around the lower leg that prevents all feeling between rider and pony.

Jodhpur straps — There are two kinds: 1) Leather straps which fit just under the knee and invariably prompt, from bystanders, the question, "Why is she wearing those leather straps?" In reply to which we ask, "Why not?", since there doesn't seem to be a better answer. Maybe it's the style and maybe they were originally introduced as a way to keep jods from bunching up or pulling down. 2) But really, the elastic straps which go under the instep, attaching by buttons or clips on either side, work well for keeping the jodhpurs in place — if, that is, you remember them. This is another easy-to-lose item. Fortunately, the elastic straps can be purchased separately from the jods.

Dorothy Henderson Pinch, *Happy Horsemanship*. (New York. Prentice Hall Press, 1966)

The Preppy, "Camera! Action!"

The Glamour Girl, "Oops"

The Barnworker

The best seat in the house

Mother's Aid

Buy several pairs just in case. It is cheaper to forget these than, say, a girth, but a pain nonetheless to hunt a pair up at the last minute. You might use a marker to initial these items. When there are six or seven pony riders from ages 7 to 14, all with straps, it's helpful to know which pair strewn on the tack room floor belong to your child.

Rainwear — This is always a necessity. A hard-hat cover is made of transparent plastic. Rubbers fit over leather boots (these function to keep the leather boots mud-free and can be removed before the child goes into the ring). Purchase a raincoat cut specially for riding.

Gloves — These should be black leather. Purchase gloves which don't bleed when wet; otherwise, when it rains the black dye gets all over everything, especially the tan breeches.

Jacket — The styles in terms of length and in-colors change. Jackets should be well-fitting, almost tight, to show off a rider's form. Wool blends breathe better than pure polyester and are lighter weight than 100% wool; personal taste, as well as the temperature of your local show season, are relevant factors. Because the picture that the child and pony make together is important, we prefer that the color of the jacket coordinate with the color of the pony's coat.

Mother's Aid

If you are uncertain about what to buy in terms of, say, color or style, attend a few shows and see how the exhibitors are dressed. Outfitting a child in show clothes involves a substantial investment and while we expect to replace outgrown show clothes, no one wants to turn around and buy a new show jacket because the one she purchased a month earlier is outdated.

Hair nets — These are, by and large, an ugly necessity (the AHSA Rule Book states that exhibitors should have a neat, workman-like appearance) and are known by the holes they breed almost before they are out of the package. Always have extras; keep one in the jacket pocket or in the lining of the hat. Two alternatives to hair nets are very, very short hair and braids. Some mothers think that braids with bows are cute. When we were weighing the pros and cons of cutting a daughter's hair, one of the deciding factors was that people commented on how cute she looked at shows with her braids and red bows. This prompted the remark from an old horse show hand that we were really becoming HSMs.

Short tail — Recently a child who crashed through a fence, and had her pony roll on her, lost her hat in the bargain. She picked herself up amid much attention from officials and mothers only to be asked by the judge, "Where's your hair net?"

Mother's Aid

In the winter months long underwear should be worn under show clothes; a chilled child can quickly become an ill child (and then who is going to exercise the pony, muck out the stall, etc.). Silk is the fabric of choice as it is not as bulky as other materials. It is easy to pull on jods over silk; they slide on with no trouble. Also, have your child try on clothes before the first winter show; otherwise you may find that the choker has become a choke-her. We found this out the hard way.

Equipment for the Warm-up Child

Sweats — They are now making sweats with leather knee pads; the oldies, baggy and colorful, are still just as popular. They are sometimes worn without socks, as in, "Oh, my legs are sore, Mom." Sweats are so bulky and stretchable that they can go on over the show outfit. The aim is always to keep the show clothes as clean as possible.

Leg wraps — The pony's leg wraps can go over the child's jeans to protect against bruises and sores by the action of jeans and stirrup leathers.

Vests — In the early morning, or at warm-ups at the winter shows, vests provide warmth while still allowing movement. However, the puffy ones can camouflage the position of the back.

Chaps — These are leather trousers made of smooth or rough skins (or a combination) and worn over other pants. They are a godsend to the compulsively neat HSM as they cover jods and keep them clean. Your child looks instantly more together wearing chaps; they're neat and keep her warm. Chaps have been known to go over shorts, jeans, jods, etc. They can be custom-made or ready-made and altered to fit; dyed any color (but be aware that dyed skins bleed when wet, i.e. when the child wears them in the rain over a pair of tan jods); and they come with or without fringe.

Hard hat — The child should *always* wear protective head gear which is properly fastened. Accidents happen, even at a walk. Calientes (colorful eventing hard hats) are often worn by the warm-up child.

The HSM and Her Equipment

This is to help you with the question of what the proper HSM wears and therefore needs to pack for the horse show. We noticed that most HSMs fall into three categories. There are Preppies, Glamour Girls and Barn Workers of America.

The Preppy — She wears a skirt, A-line or wrap-around, flowered or denim. (In cold weather chinos and a turtleneck are acceptable, as is a British waxed cotton jacket.) With it she wears a button-down blouse, possibly a kerchief, definitely topsiders or loafers. She accessorizes the

Everything but the kitchen sink . . .

" . . . a sure way to get the judge's attention!"

outfit with a sweater loosely tied around her shoulders. The hair is styled neatly, usually in a casual bob; grosgrain hair ribbons can match grosgrain watchbands and grosgrain belts. Her jewelry is minimal but real.

The Glamour Girl — She is the one you love to hate, except that she's really quite nice and very practical once you become acquainted. She tends to sit in her deck chair off to the side of the ring, just out of shouting range of the stabling. Or she maneuvers her very large car in order to watch from the comfort of its padded leather seats. She is stylishly casual in dress (expensive resort wear), with sandals, usually long hair which waves naturally. If she wears a sweatshirt it is in gold lame; if she wears a jean jacket it has fox tails swinging from the yoke. She could have a white blazer in case it gets chilly (if it's really cold she stays home) and an umbrella rather than a raincoat.

The Barn Worker — She is in jeans, T-shirt and sweatshirt (which is tied around her waist if it gets hot). She will have duckies on her feet because she knows about manure and hosing ponies down. Her hair is likely short (the wash-and-wear look that often is unwashed because there is no time) or long and tied back rather unceremoniously. If it rains she wears L.L. Bean oilcloth. She doesn't bother with an umbrella because it is impossible to hold a pony, a grooming kit, and an umbrella at the same time (plus the child's number, show jacket, and a rain sheet . . .).

Mother's Aid
Even the Barn Worker of America should pack something other than jeans. The last thing an HSM needs is to be refused admittance to a hotel dining room because she doesn't meet the dress code standard.

In our opinion HSMs should feel free to change and experiment with categories and roles . . . a preppy one day, a glamour girl the next, or a barn worker if she just can't help herself.

Accoutrements of the HSM

Dogs deserve special mention. Cats always stay home. Most horse shows demand that dogs be leashed while on the grounds. This is usually the only explicit restriction. However, one must be aware that just as the attire of the HSM creates a certain impression (Who would ask a Glamour Girl to muck out a stall?), so does the breed of a dog attached to her wrist. At the moment the breed of choice is the Jack Russell Terrier. Pembroke Welsh Corgis and West Highland White Terriers are also legitimate companions of the HSM. Hunting dogs can often pass muster although they can be too large to smuggle into hotel rooms. German Shepherds are usually tethered in the tack room. Beribboned dogs, or dogs with rhinestone collars, are questionable. If you are ever in doubt as to what breed is currently in favor with the horsey set, it is a safe bet to scan the classifieds in *The Chronicle of the Horse.*

Two Horse Show Fathers
and the Ringmaster

A Horse Show Father who
knows his place

In our opinion a full cooler is indispensible. On a hot summer day the concession stand is sure to run out of drinks; or you're between classes and the food stand is located at the other end of the showgrounds; or they do not sell your favorite beverage. Be sure to bring a cooler that is sturdy enough to sit on; there are never enough chairs to accommodate everyone.

Probably the ultimate accoutrement of the HSM is the Horse Show Father. This is a rare breed since the typical HSF works seven days a week. "Why do you think they call it the sport of kings?", one HSF asked. Or at least he always seems to be working the day of the horse show.

He can be sometimes seen holding the hand of the HSM or the too-young-to-show sibling, but seldom holding a pony.

He may come to see his child ride, but is more likely to be found *catching up on the news* with people he hasn't seen since the last show.

He's usually good about buying soda pop for thirsty riders though he's seldom there to hold a pony when they need a quick trip to the washroom.

He's either bowled over by how much better his child looks than at the last show or appalled that she's lost ground. ("What did you do to that kid?")

He's sometimes seen with his briefcase trying to figure out how to make money from horses.

He's as prone as the HSM to get too involved in wanting the child to win, and can be hard muttering to himself, "Winning isn't everything . . . winning isn't everything."

He can be seen videotaping or reading (HSFs read *The Sunday New York Times*; HSMs never seem to get a chance).

He often arrives in the nick of time with the dog, the other children, a smile of encouragement, and refreshments.

He can be seen going out to dinner with five HSMs, one being his wife.

He may be back at the motel packing and checking out because he's not as good at braiding children's hair or ponies' tails.

He may be at the motel pool. Or, like one father we know, he may be hermetically sealed in his air-conditioned car for four days.

Short tail — Even HSFs can get caught up in showing. At a recent show one HSF was overheard referring to his child by number instead of name.

It would seem that video equipment, or cameras at the very least, would be the first thing the HSM takes to a show. We, however, made the following observations about recording devices:

The HSM needs a free hand to carry the equipment.

If the HSM has her eye glued to the camera she can only see a limited aspect of her child's round.

If she focuses the camera on her own child in a flat class she will miss the rest of the class; a lot can be learned from watching the other competitors.

We learned the hard way that while the video equipment might be focused on the class in the ring, the audio component picks up remarks

Where is this father's newspaper?

HSF - Horse Show Father

"Bring a cooler sturdy enough to sit on."

A classic HSM pose

made in the general area. So, if the HSM operates such equipment, or stands near someone who is, she should be very careful about what she says.

Friends and Relatives

They are a special problem because they rarely anticipate what they are in for when they attend a horse show. Usually they are improperly dressed for the occasion (no one needs shiny loafers and a white tennis sweater at a horse show) — or, rather properly dressed which can make the HSM feel self-conscious about manure stains and dirty fingernails.

Your visitors do not accept the fact that classes are not canceled because of rain and are therefore not prepared for sudden downpours. And they are invariably the ones who slip off a plank into the mud.

Despite what they say, they came to see you and all they saw was pony after pony. They tend to want to eat at mealtimes — how very unreasonable; you eat when there is nothing else to do, which is never. They're quick to rush over to the out-gate to congratulate your child on her round (just when the trainer wants to chew her out and coach her for the next course). And they always bring cameras, wanting the child and pony to pose for just one more, usually when the trainer is waiting impatiently in the warm-up area. But since the HSM never seems to have enough time to take any pictures herself, she's the first to ask for extra prints.

The HSM is lucky if her guests are comfortable around a pony; otherwise they jump a mile when it does no more than shift its weight. But she's not so lucky if they're comfortable but not knowledgeable. These are the people who linger behind the pony's backside or feed it carrots when it's all tacked up to show.

And then there are little cousins who want pony rides (or whose mothers want them to have pony rides).

Mother's Aid
Some ponies are not of a gentle enough disposition to serve in this capacity; if yours is one, borrow a more suitable mount.

Nonetheless, it is our opinion that those friends and relatives who bother to attend shows and are willing to wait . . . and wait . . . and wait for the class to begin, deserve some sort of medal. After all, they don't have to be there. And they're usually quite supportive of their rider, leaving the criticism to the HSM and trainer. But we know of one Horse Show Grandmother who said, after observing her graddaughter's spirited application of the crop to the pony's backside, "If I'd known that's what they use crops for I wouldn't have given it to her for Christmas."

And then there are the HSM's other children. If you have several children, only one of whom shows; you are already familiar with this phenomenon. Even if you are fortunate enough to board your other

Other children at the show

children out for the show you cannot escape them, as in, "Oh my gosh, it's 7 o'clock and there are two more classes to go and I said I'd pick the other kids up at 6:30!"

The logistics of three-day shows are even more difficult. Although it may be complicated to arrange for a babysitter, shop for food, and arrange car pooling for when you're gone, consider the alternative, i.e. bringing the other children to the show. The five-year-old boy thinks it's funny to lean into the ring and shout "Boo!" The three-year-old has to go to the bathroom every five minutes. (And how can you not believe a kid who is barely toilet trained?) They are bored and want to watch cartoons — after all, it's Saturday morning. Bribery sometimes is effective, but beware of making any promises; we told one small boy he could go swimming when we returned to the hotel only to discover that the pool closed at 9 PM.

Mother's Aid

Where other children are concerned, friends and relatives can be invaluable aids to the HSM, as in, "Would you please take Johnny to the bathroom for me, I have to finish braiding this tail."

Finally, the two most important things that the HSM can bring to a show are her sense of humour and a large measure of tact. If she can laugh at herself and the various catastrophies which are sure to happen at a horse show, she has a chance to survive and tell (even write) about her experiences. And if she remembers to think before she speaks, she'll avoid an ailment (mentioned below) often associated with HSMs.

Hoof in Mouth Disease

Ponies have near sides. People have good sides.

As it is correct to mount from the near side of a pony, it is correct for an HSM to stay on the good side of people. This is not easy. We found that the pony you point out as lame is usually owned by the person standing behind you.

It has been said that the best HSM is seen but not heard. Since this is rarely possible, because most HSMs have invested untold (sometimes literally) amounts of money, time, energy and love on both pony and child, it helps to know what to say when one cannot stifle the urge to be heard. The basic guiding principle should be to accentuate the positive while downplaying (if not ignoring) the negative. In fact, when asked how the HSM should behave, one of our girls (the nine-year-old) replied, "A horse show mother should only say nice things to her own children and to the other children." We agree; there are some suggestions for those difficult situations.

When do you say when the pony just refused a fence? The prudent HSM observes that the pony must be really smart. It knew that it wasn't

72

placed right at the fence to make it over safely. It is not correct to comment: "That pony never refuses; what happened this time?" (though heaven knows you feel like saying it).

What do you say when a pony has just finished the course in record time? The mother is probably already a nervous wreck, so limit yourself to a brief, "That pony has lots of energy." Or, 'That was an exciting round."

Sometimes the opposite happens, the pony is an absolute dead-beat. You privately wonder whether the pony will make it around the course without falling asleep. It is always appropriate to murmur, "That was a nice safe round." Or, "She rode that conservatively."

Suppose the rider goes off course. Your ready reply should be, "It happens to the best of them." This has the virtue of being true.

When a child nearly runs the judge over in an under saddle class, one can say little except, "That's a sure way to get the judge's attention."

If a pony is galloping around the ring in an under saddle class (and the judge requested a canter), one might remark that it moves forward well.

There is one expression which is appropriate in many circumstances: "We're just here for the experience." When your child's green pony gets overexcited in the ring, you are just here for the experience; when she makes her complimentary circle in the wrong direction at the beginning of the over fences phase, you are just here for the experience. When she falls off her pony (in a flat class) you are just here . . .

Horse (?) play

73

Where are this HSM's pockets?

3

There's No Business Like Show Business

THIS CHAPTER IS DEDICATED to those mothers who have been handed reins (for the first time) and asked to watch the pony while its rider runs to the bathroom. Remember, you do have choices:

You can run to the bathroom first.
You can hide out with your deck chair.
You can stay home.
You can hire someone to be a groom.
You can encourage your husband (the HSF) to take your place.
You can plead ignorance, as in, "Martingale? Oh, honey, what's that?"
You can be a glamour girl. Glamour girls, after all, might chip their nail lacquer.

Barring any of the above, it's time to learn the art of holding ponies or keeping your hands in your pockets.

The Art of Holding Ponies (If You Must)

The first thing you discover is that riders are not very discriminating when they ask someone to hold their ponies; they simply pick the closest body, assuming that everyone is equal to the task. *Warning:* Under no circumstances should you agree to hold the horse of a stranger for *just a few minutes* while she runs into the enty tent or the bathroom. You know nothing about the horse's behavior or idiosyncracies. It is no matter that ten minutes passed and your child's class was just announced; you remain tethered to the beast until relieved by the relieved rider.

Holding ponies

Should you fail to keep your hands in your pockets and agree to hold a pony, the following measures should be taken:

Hold the lead shank (or, if the pony is wearing a bridle, pull the reins over its head and hold them as one) about six inches from the pony's chin in your right.

Stand next to the left side of the pony, at about the level of its head and shoulder, facing forward.

At the same time, hold the end of the lead shank (or the reins) in your left hand, so that neither you nor the pony get entangled.

As a safety measure (for yourself), never wrap the end of the lead shank (or reins) around your hand. You are now prepared if the pony decides to move on.

What if the pony won't stand still? First, try to calm it with a few reassuring, quiet words. If this doesn't work, turn it in a circle and then stop, saying "Whoa" firmly. When it stops, reward it with a pat. If you are standing in a grassy area the pony may want to graze. Do not permit a pony with a bit in its mouth to eat; if it starts to graze, pull the head up. Sometimes a quick, sharp jerk of the reins is required. If the pony is persistent, you might want to move away from the grassy area. However, if the pony is all groomed for showing, avoid moving to either muddy ground or dusty areas.

Warning: — Since a pony's mouth can be wet and slimy, watch out that it doesn't slobber all over your outfit. Some ponies bite, especially when bored.

Leading Ponies

It is said that you can lead a horse to water but you can't make it drink. Some of us cannot even lead it to water. Leading a pony is not terribly difficult once you know how:

Hold the pony as suggested above.

Looking ahead, calmly and confidently walk forward. (Calmness and confidence are respected by ponies.) Be sure to stay beside its left shoulder and head; if you walk in front of the should you may find yourself right in its path. Also, if you get ahead of the pony you may find yourself pulling on the head, which can cause it to resist.

If the pony won't follow you:

Do not turn and look it in the eye. For some reason when you turn around to look at ponies, they become even more stubborn about moving forward.

Try a little child psychology on the beast. Brute force is ineffective unless your physical capabilities are truly unique. Sometimes just speaking

Riders with their numbers displayed

"Don't forget your number."

to it helps as long as you sound confident and self-assured. Probably the most effective trick is to turn it in a circle and then go forward in the direction desired. We don't know whether this works because it alters the pony's balance or simply because it distracts the pony, but it does work. Once it's moving, keep it moving. Walking briskly is a good sign to the pony that you mean to keep going forward.

Stopping the pony:
Usually when you stop it will stop. Occasionally it won't. Say "Whoa" and stand firm. You may want to give a sharp tug or two on the leadline or reins. If the pony still wants to move forard, turn it in a circle and then stop. Yelling or screaming merely excites it; threatening makes you look the fool. Confine yourself to muttering under your breath.

Playing the Numbers

In addition to holding and walking ponies, HSMs are delegated as keepers-of-the-numbers. Every rider must exhibit her competition number. The AHSA Rule Book clearly states that numbers must be worn on a rider's back and be visible at all times. This means that a rider can be eliminated from the competition if the number is displayed incorrectly or not at all.

At a recent show the exhibitors were permitted to wear rain gear because of the inclement weather. One child was eliminated from a pony hunter class because her number, although fastened to the back of her hunt coat, was obscured by her raincoat.

Your first job is to take possession of the number, which can be picked up at the entry desk (provided your entries are complete). You will find that your child is assigned a number for each pony she rides.

Mother's Aid
If your child is riding more than one pony write the name of the pony on the back of the number, so that you can keep track of which number goes with which pony.

Even as simple a task as securing a number to the rider's back can become complicated. Since the aim is to present a *pleasing picture* in the ring, it should come as no surprise that one never simply pins the number to the back of the coat. Consider first the card that the number is printed on; it is either circular or rectangular. The former looks more attractive on a rider; if you have the opportunity to alter the shape of the rectangular card, do so. For instance, you can round the corners of the card. Or sometimes the number on a rectangular card is surrounded by a printed circle. This is an invitation to convert the rectangle to a circle. Whatever you choose to do, do it as neatly and unobtrusively as possible.

ADD/SCRATCH

Entry #_____   Entry Name_____

                       Trainer_____

                       Owner _____

                       Rider _____

Add Class_____ ‖ Scratch Class_____

Date _____ Signature _____

Add/Scratch Form

Mother's Aid

It is helpful to have scissors in your bag. We remember well a horse show where (having had strict instructions from the trainer to cut the number) we spent numerous valuable minutes asking numerous people if they had scissors.

Many numbers are designed with clips that fasten to the exhibitor's collar. This places the number too high on the back and interferes with the rider's equitation. Ignore the clips, punch holes on either side of the number, and tie it on. This permits you to secure the number lower on the rider's back. It helps if you bring a holepunch and a long string (preferably one that blends with the hunt coat) to shows. We use shoelaces, although braiding yarn of a dark color also works.

Warning — At one of the first horse shows it was announced that second place in a short stirrup class had been awarded to number 99. "Unfortunately," the announcer continued, we have no information on number 99." A few minutes later the announcer informed the crowd that 99's number was 66! Number 99 has never let one of the authors forget this incident. Subsequently we discovered that the number of the horse is often printed, along with the entered classes, on the back of the number. So, before you secure the number to the back of the rider be sure that it is right-side up; your reputation as an HSM is at stake.

Probably the hardest thing about numbers is keeping track of them, especially at a three- or four-day show. We suggest a designated spot — the jacket bag, the grooming kit, the hook on the stall door — where the number is to be placed as soon as it is taken off. There is no panic (well almost none) equal to that of a competitor whose class is being called and who cannot find her number.

Horse Show Math

You might be asked to add or scratch an entry. To add, go to the entry desk and fill out an *add* form. You need to know the exhibitor's number, the number of the class being entered, the show name of the pony, and the name of the ownest) entries, those made after the closing date. Information about them can be found in the Prize List.

When you scratch a pony from a class you are officialy removing it. To do this, complete a *scratch* form at the entry desk. Again, you need the same information that you use to add an entry. You will not need your checkbook, however. In fact, if you can show that the pony cannot compete because of illness or injury, you may be entitled to the return of your entry fee. Again, check the Price List for the rules governing this.

"I'll have a decaf!"

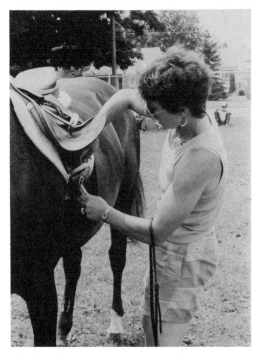

Buckling the girth after removing the martingale

Cleaning mud from the tail for the jog

Applying hoof dressing

83

Mother's Aid
It is helpful to carry a list of classes in which your children are entered, especially at a four-day show.

Jot down on the back of the number the classes in which your rider will compete. Or you may (in confusion, like one mother we know) send your child into a class, only to discover that she wasn't registered in it. You could find yourself racing to the secretary's booth and hurriedly *adding* the class.

Drug Testing

The AHSA maintains strict drug standards. It forbids the use of any stimulant, depressant, tranquilizer, or local anesthetic which might affect the performance of the pony, as well as the use of other drugs which mask the detection of these drugs.

As a means of enforcing these regulations, recognized shows include in the entry fee a charge of $4 for each pony. This fee subsidizes the AHSA-sponsored drug testing program. Any animal entered in the show can be subject to these examinations. If your pony is chosen to be tested, do not panic; this does not mean that the officials suspect your pony has been illegally drugged. Some of the animals are selected randomly.

One of our daughters attending her first AHSA-recognized show wanted to know why her pony couldn't be tested (After all, we paid.). This daughter was well prepared for any eventuality; a couple of days earlier she admonished us not to give her pony any of our cola, saying, "There'll be caffeine in her bloodstream when they test her for drugs at the show!" We had a good laugh over this, only to read more recently a warning not to let ponies drink pop with caffeine in it because it shows up in a drug test. Out of the mouths of babes . . .

If your pony is selected to participate in the drug-testing program, an official will tell you where to take the animal for the test (which can consist of samples of urine, saliva, and blood). The AHSA urges you to be as helpful as possible, as much for your benefit as everyone else's. One of our ponies was selected randomly to be tested for drugs. The rider and mother accompanied the veterinarian and the pony back to the stall for the test. It turned out that a urine sample was required. With the pony on cross-ties outside the stall, we all stood around waiting for some output. We waited . . . and waited . . . and waited. After about forty minutes, the rider asked the veterinarian, "Why don't we just put the pony in the stall? It goes as soon as you do." And it did.

Not only must you cooperate in procuring the sample, but you must not hinder the collection. You should be aware that the AHSA forbids any

84

Clean-up committee

When does the HSM get her
bubble bath?

delays such as schooling, lengthy cooling out, and bandaging. Bear in mind that, although collecting the sample may be a nuisance, the drug testing program protects the competitor in that all ponies are bound by the same restrictions in terms of drug use. Regulation of drug use also protects the animals.

Stagemanaging the Props or Tacking Up

Rest assured that someday you will be asked to saddle and bridle a pony. Although we can provide simple guidelines for these tasks, you should be initiated into the art of tacking up before you arrive at a show — ten minutes before a class starts is not the ideal time to practice. Also, it is much easier to learn how to saddle and bridle a horse if you watch someone else do it first.

To put the halter on:
Place the noseband over the muzzle.
Slip the headpiece over the ears, one ear at a time.
Fasten the buckle on the cheek-piece.
Tie up the pony with a slip knot, or put it on cross-ties.
Warning — Do not omit that last step; if you had to return to the tack room for a girth or martingale, it would be dangerous to leave the pony loose. This applies to even the most docile; any animal can behave *out of character* if, says, someone zooms by on a motorcycle or a cat leaps on its back.

Saddle-ing:
Approach the pony from the near side (left side).
Place the saddle pad slightly in front of the withers. The pad must fit evening on the back without any wrinkles; otherwise the pony will get sores. Place the saddle, with the stirrups run up, gently on the saddle pad (again, approach from the near side). Slide both the pad and saddle back until they are positioned correctly (slightly behind the withers). Always move the saddle from front to back to ensure that the hairs on the pony lie in the correct direction.
If you've placed the saddle and pad too far back, lift them off the pony's back and reposition them — do not slide them up.
Once the position is correct, check to be sure that the pad is smooth and evenly placed under the saddle. For adequate ventilation, push the pad up into the pommel area. This make a conduit for air to flow between the pony and the saddle.
Attach the pad to the saddle.
Fasten the girth on the off side, then on the near side.
The girth should be snug. The rider will check and tighten the girth, if necessary before mounting.

86

HSM at ringside with the grooming kit

HSM grooming the child

87

Bridle-ing:

Approach from the near side.

Remove the halter and buckle it around the pony's neck.

Place the headpiece of the bridle over *your* left shoulder.

Put the reins over the pony's head.

Hold the bridle with the headpiece in your right hand and the bit in your left.

Gently put the bit in the pony's mouth (try not to knock its teeth). A well-trained pony will open its mouth when it feels the bit against its lips, but if it doesn't . . . slip your finger in the side of its mouth, where it doesn't have any teeth.

Once the bit is in place, put the headpiece over its ears, one at a time.

Pull the forelock over the brow band and buckle the noseband and the throat latch. Allow about two fingers between the noseband and the pony's jaw; you should be able to fit about three fingers between the throat latch and the head.

Move in front of the pony and look at the bridle, making sure that it is properly placed and not crooked.

Then place all of the straps in their keepers (dangling straps can distract the pony and are not favored by judges).

Remove the halter when the pony is bridled and ready to move or be mounted.

Warning — Never leave a pony tied up for very long.

Mother's Aid
In the winter, warm the bit in your hand (or blow on it).

De-bridle-ing:

Approach the pony from the near side.

Before you remove the bridle, fasten a halter around the pony's neck. This will help your control if it decides to move on.

Pull the reins over its head and unfasten the throat latch and noseband.

Gently slip the headpiece over the ears with your right hand and catch the bit in the left hand.

Once the bridle has been removed, drape it over your left shoulder and put the halter on the pony.

Be sure that the pony is securely tied and then put the bridle away.

Warning — Never drop the bridle on the ground; aside from the fact that damp ground is not the ideal resting place for a bridle, you do not want either yourself or the animal to trip over the reins.

De-saddle-ing:

With the pony still tied, you can remove the saddle.

Run up the stirrups.

Sally's Salon

Unwrapping the pony's legs

Unbuckle the girth buckles on the near side.

Move to the off side and unbuckle the girth buckles.

Remove the girth and place it across the seat of the saddle. Don't let the girth bang against the animal's legs: the tendons and ligaments in the lower legs are unprotected and vulnerable to bruising. Think about how it feels when you bang your ankles or shins.

Return to the nearside and lift (do not drag) the saddle and pad off the animal's back.

Be sure that you put the saddle away carefully. Many show saddles are made of smooth, fine bridle leather which is easily scratched.

Grooming the Pony

According to Webster's, a groom is a man or boy whose work is tending, feeding, and currying horses. Webster notwithstanding, the typical HSM is neither a man or a boy, yet she is often a groom. We found that if the HSM looks the part (dressed, say, in jeans and sweatshirt) she is often called on to play it. Few HSMs decked out in sandals, designer clothes and a Gucci bag are expected to brush a pony. Hmmm... the well-groomed HSM is NOT asked to groom the pony while the poorly-groomed HSM is seldom seen without a rub rag and body brush.

First put the halter on and then either put the pony on cross-ties or tie it up with a slip knot. Be sure that the grooming equipment is assembled nearby. You need (minimally) a currycomb, hard brush, soft brush, rub rag, hoof pick, baby oil, fly spray, hoof dressing, and sponge.

Picking out the feet is the first step. To pick out the front feet, stand next to the pony's shoulder, facing the rear end. Run your hand down the back of its leg until you reach the fetlock; then gently pull up. If the pony doesn't lift its foot, lean against the shoulder; this puts its weight on the opposite leg.

When the pony raises its foot, support it with one hand while you clean it out with the other. With the hoof pick clean from the back to the front. Be sure to clean out the cleft of the frog, i.e. the deep grooves.

To clean out the rear feet, stand next to the hindquarters and run your hand down the back of each leg. Proceed as for the front feet.

Picking out the feet may not make the pony look better, but it makes it go better. If a foreign object is lodged in the hoof, a bruise would eventually form and the pony could go lame. Just think about how you feel when a stone is in your shoe. While you are cleaning the feet, check to be sure that each shoe is tight and that no nails are loose.

Use the currycomb in a circular motion around the body except for the areas which are bony. You can use a rubbr curry mitt, gently, on the bony parts of the body: legs, face, etc. Check the currycomb periodically to be sure that it is not getting clogged; it can be cleaned by rubbing it against a hard brush or by hitting it against a hard suface (like a stall door).

The currycomb only works the dirt loose. You brush the dirt off the pony with the hard brush. Brush in the direction of the hair. Do not use the hard brush on the face or any other sensitive area. Ponies differ regarding this; some can tolerate a hard brush on the belly, while others cannot. Be sensitive to the animal you're grooming; the hard brush can indeed be very harsh. A dirty brush cannot clean a pony; clean the brush by rubbing it against the currycomb.

The soft brush can now be used on the body. Use circular, firm (gentle around sensitive areas) strokes in the same direction that the hair grows. Since the purpose is to reach the skin of the pony and stimulate circulation while cleaning the coat, you really need to put some weight behind your brushing.

Clean the soft brush by rubbing it against the currycomb.

Now you can clean the mane and tail with the soft brush, although you should clean out the tail by hand if it is at all thin — the brush can break off hairs. Brush the mane so that it falls on the offside. Unfasten the halter and refasten it around the pony's neck. Then you can brush the face, being sure to do the ears. Be gentle because this is a very bony and sensitive area.

Rubbing the pony with a cactus cloth, rub rag, or towel helps make the coat shiny. The rubbing stimulates circulation and brings the oil to the surface of the coat.

With a wet sponge clean around the eyes, mouth, and nostrils (both the inside and outside). Rewet the sponge and then lift the tail and clean the entire area around the dock. Although the sheath and penis should be cleaned periodically, this need not be done every time the pony enters the show ring. Let your child, trainer, or veterinarian attend to this matter at some more appropriate time. This is definitely not part of the HSM's job description.

Clean the hooves with a hard brush. Then apply a thin coat of hoof oil to the heel and hoof, up to the coronet. Since hoof oil readily picks up dirt, you might want to wait to apply this at ringside, moments before your competitors enters. This looks best if applied carefully. Sometimes HSMs are more meticulous than trainers.

Finally, apply baby oil around the eyes and muzzle. Use a very small amount of oil, as it tends to attract dirt and dust. The oil draws attention to the pony's face by making the coat shiny. If needed, apply fly repellant. Do not spray the fact; rather, wipe it on with a cloth.

The pony is now ready to show. Do not, however, suppose that it will maintain this condition between the barn and the show ring. Take a modified grooming kit to the ring. We recommend a container, with a handle, stocked with: a brush, rub rag (to use on the pony), rub rag (to use on the rider's boots), fly spray (just in case), hoof oil, and a sponge to re-clean the nostrils and muzzle. If the weather is threatening, throw in rain gear for the rider and pony. You might want to include a cooler and fly

Loading the trailer

sheet; these can be used between classes and after the competition is completed.

You realize, of course, that someone is needed at the show ring to attend to last-minute tune-ups. Now you know why golf carts are standard equipment for HSMs.

On the Road Again

Shipping bandages protect the pony's legs in transit. Since the amount of protectin provided is a function not only of the quality of the bandages used, but also of the quality of the wrapping job, be meticulous when you wrap a pony's legs. The quilts must be *thick* to afford proper protection.

Over a pad (or quilt) wrap the bandage from just below the knee all the way down to the hoof and then back up again. Wrap counter-clockwise on the left legs and clockwise on the right legs. When bandaging pull the leg wrap snugly around the front of the leg and *lay* it around the back of the leg. If the bandage is pulled tightly across the back of the leg it can cause a knot in the tendon called *cording*. Although it may look sloppy, be sure to pad and bandage the junction between the hoof and the hair line, a vulnerable area.

The bandage must be secure enough to stay in position, but not so tight that it jeopardizes the circulation. One or two fingers should be able to fit between the bandage and leg. And if, for instance, the leg wraps start slipping as you walk the pony to the trailer, they are too loose. If the bandages slip out of position, then the animal's legs won't be protected during the trip. Many accidents and injuries occur because improperly wrapped ponies often panic when things get tangled around their legs.

Mother's Aid
Set aside 30 minutes if you are not experienced at wrapping legs. It always takes longer than you think and everyone else will be anxious to get on the road.

Bandages are either fastened by velcro or tied. If you have to tie the tapes, be sure that the bow either falls on the outside or the inside of the leg. If it falls on the front, then it would rub against a bone; if it falls on the back, then it would rub against a tendon. We found that securing the bandages or wraps with masking tape adds an extra measure of security. We have known ponies en route to undo wraps, lead ropes, and even take off halters — dumb beasts, my eye!

Warning — Always maintain a posture which enables you to move quickly out of the pony's way. We have seen children kneeling on the ground beside their ponies when they wrap the legs; one girl even sat on the

The trailer loaded

ground. This may be comfortable, especially at four in the morning, but it's very dangerous.

Since many ponies rub their tails, resulting in broken-off hairs which not only look like a rat's nest but also make braiding impossible, it is helpful to apply a tail bandage. Wet the tail first. Then, lifting the tail with one hand, wrap the bandage around the top of the tail twice to secure it (no quilt is used). Keep wrapping, stopping just before the end of the tailbone. The bandage must be wrapped tightly enough so that it will stay on but must not be so tight that it cuts off the circulation. We now of at least one pony whose tail fell off because the bandage was wrapped too tightly and left on too long. Only practice will tell you the degree of tightness required; it is better to be too loose than too tight since you only risk the bandage falling off in the former case.

Mother's Aid
Some people recommend turning a few of the tail hairs up while you are wrapping. If you do this several times, the bandage will remain secure.

To unwrap the legs, simiply unfasten the wraps and unwind. Don't bother re-rolling the bandages at this point. Just pay attention where you drop the leg wraps; if you lay them in a snowbank or a puddle, then you will have less-than-desirable materials to rewrap the pony for shipment home.

Do not unwrap the tail bandage to remove it; simply unfasten it and, holding it with both hands near the dock, slide it down and off.

Do not provide water in the trailer. Most people hang a haynet in the trailer; do this before you load the animals.

Warning — Be sure the haynet is hung in such a way that there is no danger of the animal entangling its legs in it. You should secure the already full haynet so that the hay is about level with the eyes to minimize the danger of the pony catching its feet. However, don't be overzealous in your concern and hang the haynet any higher than eye level. You also need to minimize the amount of dust and bits of hay getting into the pony's eyes.

If you've never been asked to help load a pony, you're lucky. You can be sure that this is not a permanent reprieve and that someday you will participate. With a halter and lead shank, quietly walk your pony to the ramp. Don't rush, ponies need time to understand what you want them to do. But act confidently. Willingness to load is partly a measure of the animal's confidence in the human leading it into the trailer. For this reason, if you feel nervous or scared about leading a pony into a trailer, let someone else do it since the pony will sense your fear.

HSM loading the pony

The ponies loaded

Warning — An HSM was recently loaded by a hungry pony who was anxious to get to the haynet in the trailer.

After you've led the pony inside, have someone else waiting to put the chain up and shut the tailgate, or ramp (so the pony cannot back off). Once the chain, or bar, is fastened, tie the pony up with a slipknot. You should not do this before the chain is fastened because the pony may attempt to back up and, finding itself secured, try to break free.

You will quickly find that it is difficult to drag an unwilling pony into a trailer. There are several techniques for handling this situation. It helps if a willing pony, one that loads easily, goes first. do not have your pony watch a reluctant loader; this will only compound the problem. leave it in the barn until the unwilling one is loaded.

It sometimes helps if a difficult pony is lightly touched on the rump with a broom or rake. For some reason it is usually the unsuspecting HSM who is asked to wield the implements of persuasion. For your own safety remain alert and take special care not to get trapped between the pony and the side of the trailer. Always stand to the side of the animal — they all kick! If the pony is very difficult to load, you can put a rope behind it with one person on each end, pushing forward.

When unloading, if your trailer unloads from the front, put down the ramp, open the door, untie the pony, remove the front chain, or bar, and lead the pony down the ramp.

To unload from the back, reach in through the escape door and untie the pony. You can just throw the lead shank over its neck. Then open the back door and remove the chair, or bar. Someone must be standing nearby to guide it down off the ramp and to take hold of the lead shank. Ponies often back off quite quickly, so this person must be alert.

Unwilling loaders are usually uwilling unloaders, but if you have a problem, reach in through the escape door and gently push on the pony's chest and say, "Go back" or "Back up" (or something to that effect).

" . . . got left at the 6th fence."

4

Good "Mudders" and Bad "Mudders"

AT ONE OF OUR FIRST horse shows we asked why our child didn't pin, i.e. get a ribbon. The instructor answered, "Although she met the first three fences well, she chipped in at the fourth, didn't get a full lead change after the fifth, got left at the sixth, added a stride between the sixth and seventh, and dropped the pony at the last one."

This chapter is dedicated to the HSM who *got left* at the fourth fence.

Since many of our early frustrations stemmed from the fact that we had no idea what the judges were looking at in the various classes, we decided that this book would not be complete without some explanation of what they expect from the ponies and riders and what distinguishes a good ride from a bad one. We hope that this chapter helps you understand how a particular class might be pinned. HSMs may never reach the level of expertise of their children's trainer, but they can become intelligent observers. And while there are no ribbons awarded to HSMs, their performance and equitation does not go unnoticed.

How to Watch a Hunter Class Over Fences or the Ins and Outs of Classes Over Fences

What is the judge looking at in a performance class over fences? The rider and pony enter the ring at a walk or a trot. She makes a courtesy circle, picking up a canter to establish the pace. She then negotiates the pre-established course, ending with another circle. The pony is judged on soundness, performance, manners, and suitability for the rider.

Soundness — By AHSA rules, ponies entered in performance classes over fences must be serviceably sound. A pony that is not sound will not be in the ribbons.

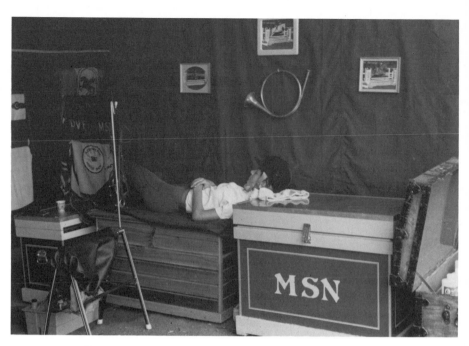

The princess and the pea wouldn't survive a horse show.

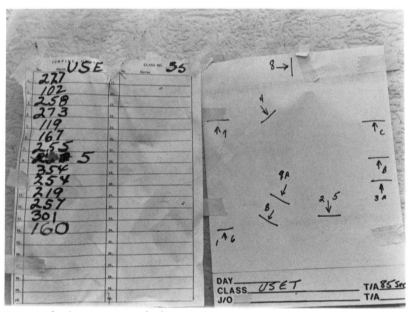

Diagram of a hunter course - don't you wish it were a map showing which way to the beach!

When the over fences phase is completed, the top ponies are *jogged* back, with the rider dismounted and the saddle, pad, and martingale removed, to test for soundness. At the in-gate you will see lots of people madly polishing the pony. According to the AHSA, an unsound pony is one who shows signs of lameness, broken wind, or blindness. Soundness is emphasized in hunter divisions because a hunter class is supposed to simulate the conditions of a hunt; an unsound pony would be inappropriate.

Performance — Performance refers to the way the animal negotiates the course, not only over the fences but between the fences. Ideally the pony maintains an even and correct (for the fences) pace, bending on the turns, approaching the middle of the fence on a straight line, maintaining it in the air, and then continuing it upon landing. The pony finds the proper spot for take-off and jumps athletically (back and neck rounded, knees snapped up).

The performance of the HSM is measured by how many people — child, trainer, other mothers, family — are still speaking to her at the end of a division.

Pace — Ideally the pony's pace is consistent throughout the course and appropriate for the size of the fences. For this reason a small animal (especially one with a short stride) may have to maintain a quicker pace than a larger one in order to meet the fences correctly. A smaller animal may appear to be *rushing*, which occurs when a pony is moving around the course at an excessive rate of speed. A pony might maintain a nice steady pace, only to rush when it approaches a fence on a straight line.

Pace is also important to the HSM. If she starts early enough to get ready for the show (making lists, doing the laundry, sending in forms) she will avoid some of the rushing associated with early morning take-off for shows. She also needs to pace herself throughout the show if she hopes to make it to the last class. Naps are encouraged; horse trailers have been known to accommodate swinging hammocks as well as swaying ponies. And tack trunks are a popular alternative.

Course — A diagram of the sequence of jumps and lines that make up a course is posted (usually on a bulletin board) before the class begins. Any deviation from this results in elimination, the rider being *off course*.

Riding the straight and narrow — This occurs when the rider and pony maintain a straight line for the approach, jump, and landing. The line should fall through the middle of the fence. A pony is said to *weave* when its approach is crooked; *drift* when its path through the air is off the straight line.

Refusals

The HSM must also keep to the straight and narrow. This means not saying the wrong thing to the wrong person at the wrong time. It also suggests a certain level of deportment. The expectations of the show child can be quite high, with regard to the HSM's demeanor. We know of at least one child who met her HSM at the hotel room door one night with, "Where have you been? Do you know what time it is? You know that I have to show tomorrow!"

Bending — While ponies are supposed to stay straight on the straight lines, they are supposed to bend on turns. This means that the entire body of the pony bends the way that it is moving on the turn. Bending is important for maintaining balance. A pony is said to *bulge* when it drops its shoulder to the outside through the turn; it is not bending.

The HSM is said to bulge when she visits the food stand too frequently. Flexibility is also a trait desired in HSMs and children. HSMs are often asked to bend. They are asked to bend the rules. They bend over to retrieve dropped crops, polish boots, and pick out hooves. And they bend over backwards to get along with children, trainers, husbands, ponies, and, finally, other HSMs.

It is also helpful if the children are flexible and recognize that HSMs are people too. The HSM may want to attend the exhibitor's party (and return to the hotel after curfew) or relax in a bubble bath rather than hose down a pony.

Refusals — When a pony refuses a jump, it does not even try to take off; it stops. This is penalized heavily because of the potential danger it represents for the rider. A *run-out* occurs when the pony not only refuses the jump, but runs off the path of the fence, i.e. ducks away from the fence.

HSMs may refuse — in fact, at times, it saves everyone's sanity, as in, "No, you may not go swimming tonight; warm-up is at 6:00 AM."

Finding the spot — This refers to the pony's ability to take off from the correct spot. Ideally the pony takes off and lands at equidistant spots from the fence. The ideal take-off spot depends on the size of the fence, the pace established, and the animal's stride and abilities. A pony is *under the fence* when it takes off too close. This is also called a *short spot*. This is not desirable in a hunter pony, because it has to compensate by relying on greater forward thrust from the rear, or hocks, in order for the forward legs to clear the obstacle safely. Not all ponies are athletic enough to accommodate short spots safely. A pony finds a *long spot* when it takes off too far from the fence. Under these circumstances it might not be able to clear the fence; it could either crash into the obstacle or bring down rails with the front or rear end. Bringing down rails with the front legs is the more serious fault as it is more dangerous; if the front legs get entangled in the fence, the pony could go down on its knees. It is only the athletic pony that can compensate for a long spot by jumping higher (so that it lands a safe distance from the jump) and thereby avoiding *knock-downs*. Knock-downs occur when the animal brings down part of the obstacle, usually a rail. A *rub* occurs when a portion of the fence is ticked by the pony.

Safety is a main consideration for judging standards and the AHSA Rule Book mandates that unsafe jumping be penalized. If a pony meets a fence poorly, i.e. takes a short or a long spot, then the rider's safety is compromised. An *honest* pony may meet a fence poorly but, rather than refuse it, will try to find a way to get the rider over safely. It also helps if the pony is athletic, i.e. in addition to having a *heart* it also has the ability to get out of a tight spot. Such an animal is talented. If it meets the fence at a short spot, it can rock back to get the weight off its front end and engage its hocks to gain thrust from the hind end. A pony *engages its hocks* when it lowers down on the hocks and pushes off with its hind end, taking the weight off the front. If faced with a long spot it can overjump the fence, i.e. jump higher than the size of the fence would normally dictate so that it clears the obstacle safely.

For HSMs, finding the spot refers to finding the show grounds, the camp grounds, the motel — and maybe even the night spot.

Ponies *use themselves well* when they arch the neck and back over a jump while snapping the legs up so that they appear to be tightly folded. *Dangling legs* (or *hanging legs*) are not folded up so that the forelimbs are dangerously close to the fence. This compromises the rider's safety and is penalized by the judges.

It has been said that some ponies have a certain natural ability to use themselves well. Some HSMs also have a natural talent for controlling temper and emotions, juggling six things at once, and are not, furthermore, intimidated by the judges, ponies, children, trainers and weather. Such an HSM is said to use herself well.

Lead changes — Ponies are supposed to negotiate turns on the correct lead. They can either land, after a fence, on the correct lead or make a *flying lead change*. This occurs when the pony changes its leading leg at the moment when all four legs are off the ground during the canter. A *complete lead change* results when the pony achieves the correct lead in back and front. If it only picks up the correct lead in the front, then the canter is called a *cross canter*. This is very clumsy-looking and can unbalance the pony, making it difficult to maintain a steady, smooth pace; it may shorten its stride or increase its pace, especially in the corners, to compensate for the lack of balance. When the pony does this, it is said to be *scrambling*.

If the pony maintains an incorrect lead, both back and front, then it is holding a *counter canter*. While this is not a disjointed canter, per se, it still unbalances the pony, especially in turns or corners.

A bedraggled spectator

The show must go on . . .

Raingear for a VCR

Counting the strides (or horse show math) — The hunter course is designed with a specific number of strides between the fences on a line. For instance, an *in and out* consists of two fences set one stride apart. In order to cover the distance between the fences in the correct number of strides, the pony may need to adjust its stride. Hence, you often hear instructors shouting, "It's a *forward* 5!" (or, "It's a *long* 5!"), meaning that the pony needs to be moved up more; or, "It's a *steady* 4!" (or, "It's a *nice* 4!"), meaning that the pony needs to continue at the same pace; or, "It's a *waiting* 5!" (or, "It's a *short* 5!"), meaning that the pony needs to be *backed off* (or held in).

Adjusting the pace of the pony affects the length of stride. Some ponies, however, are naturally *short-strided*, i.e. the maximum length of their stride is on the short side. (The ideal stride for large ponies is 12 feet, for small to medium ponies, 10-11 feet.) Short-strided ponies have difficulty in *making the distance* because their stride cannot be lengthened sufficiently. A pony *adds a stride* when it covers the distance in one more stride than is correct (although what is correct may depend on the footing — if the ground is slick, the trainer may want the child to ride conservatively and add a stride). Sometimes the pony adds the stride evenly, i.e. the distance is covered in an equal number of strides. Sometimes it even adds more than one stride. And a pony can also leave out strides.

Often when the pony adds a stride it *chips in* by adding a shorter stride just before the fence. This is also called *cheating* at some barns. If ponies are not *supported* by their riders they will often chip in. We say that a rider is not supporting her pony when she has insufficient contact with the mouth and is not encouraging the pony with a steady leg. In order to get over a fence the pony must not only be moving forward but also in an upward motion. A rider must contact with the mouth in order to steady the pony and lighten the forehand so that the thrust comes from the hocks. A pony that is *heavy on the forehand* is not using its rear end enough. This is not good because the engine is in the rear of the pony.

The HSM can also be said to chip in. She chips in her *two sense* (which can tempt the trainer to throw away the HSM. She chips in her *two cents* (which, unfortunately, amounts to a whole lot more than two cents).

And while we say that some ponies are *heavy on the forehand*, we say that some HSMs are *heavy-handed*. According to Webster's, a heavy-handed HSM is tactless or tyrannical; this can refer to her relations with her child, her child's trainer, the pony, her family, and other HSMs.

More horse show match Horse show math is a lot like the new math that plagued a generation of parents. Simple addition and subtraction became incomprehensible . . . how else can you account for giving your child a five dollar bill for a coke and hamburger at a horse show and get nothing in return? And consider counting, as in counting the strides. Is a

106

HSM to child: "Did you pack your raincoat?"

Lunch break

"Throwing away the pony"

short 5 equal to a forward 6? Does a steady 4 equal a long 3? Is a waiting 2 plus a forward 3 equal to a steady 4?

Overjumping — A fence is overjumped when the pony clears it by an overly wide margin. This occurs when, say, the pony's jump was sufficient to clear a four-foot obstacle but it as jumping an eighteen inch cross-rail. If a pony meets the fence at a long spot, it may overjump the fence in order to land sufficiently clear of the obstacle. A fence can also be overjumped by the rider. As an example, consider the rider who makes a big move forward when the fence is an eighteen inch cross-rail. This is not needed and looks ridiculous.

Throwing away the pony — When a rider throws away the pony she doesn't support the pony to the fence; she has very light contact with the mouth and releases the head and neck too soon. The head and neck represent a significant portion of the pony's total weight. If the pony is not supported at the jump, the head and neck drop, increasing the weight on the forehand. This, in turn, makes the obstacle more difficult for the pony to clear. Often, when the rider throws the pony away, she is *ahead of the motion*, i.e. her center of gravity is ahead of the pony's center of gravity.

After three days of showing in the rain the HSM can be forgiven for thinking, just momentarily, of throwing away the pony.

Overfacing and *underfacing* — These terms apply to either rider or animal. Riders and ponies are overfaced when they are asked to jump an obstacle which is beyond their capabilities. Besides being dangerous, this can sour the children — and the ponies. They will be *turned off*, i.e. lack the heart for it. Riders and ponies are underfaced when they face jumps which are really too elementary for their abilities.

The HSM is overfaced when too many things happen too fast. She is seldom underfaced.

Elimination — According to the AHSA Rule Book, a rider is excused from an over fences competition if:
  a) The animal bolts from ring.
  b) The animal goes off course.
  c) The animal jumps an obstacle not included in course.
  d) A fence is jumped before it is reset.
  e) There have been three refusals.
  f) Either rider or pony fall while competing.

Important note: The HSM or trainer may eliminate a child from competition if her behavior becomes intolerable.

Footing — Either it rains or it doesn't rain at a horse show. If it doesn't rain and the ground is very dry, the surface can become hard and unyielding, like concrete. Constant pounding on this surface can be hard on the pony's legs. When it rains it produces mud which can be slick, causing the pony to slip and lose its balance. Thick mud creates its own problems. If you've ever walked through it to get a pony out of a pasture (and lost a rubber boot), you have experienced the same footing that a pony faces in a muddy ring. And mud is just as hard on horseshoes as human shoes except that when a pony loses a shoe in the mud, we say that it *pulled a shoe.*

Good Mudders and Bad Mudders — Good mudders are ponies that can show for three days in the rain, in lousy footing, and perform well. Bad mudders just don't do well when the footing is poor; they slip, switch leads because they're trying to keep their balance, and can't maintain a proper pace.

It is our opinion that HSMs who perform well for three days in the rain, in lousy footing, are more than good mudders. They are saints.

Fences — Ideally the course is a test of a hunter. Therefore, the fences are supposed to simulate natural fences that might be found in a hunting field. They might include a stone or brick wall, picket fence, gate, chicken coop, brush, post and rail, etc. The height of the fences and the distance of the spreads is given in the show's Prize List.

The fences can be set up a specific distance apart on a straight line. This arrangement tests the pony's ability to negotiate the obstacles without deviating from a straight line (either on the ground or in the air) while covering the distance between the fences in the correct number of strides. Fences can also be separated by a *broken line,* i.e. no straight line between them. This tests the pony's ability to turn, change leads, and jump from an angle (which tempts him to run-out). While fences set on a straight line generally have an optimum number of strides in which to be negotiated, a broken line can be ridden in several ways.

Manners — In addition to soundness and performance the AHSA Rule Book requires judges to take into account the pony's manners and its suitability for the rider. This means that the height and weight of the chid should, in turn, be suitable to the size of the pony. AHSA regulations also state that extreme speed should be penalized. The pony's manners are considered because one concern in equestrian activities is that the animal be appropriately matched to the rider's abilities. It would not, for instance, be safe to mount a child on a *hot* pony, i.e.. one which bucks around the ring, startles easily, rears, or refuses fences.

A child who makes unreasonable demands, cries at the drop of a hat, moans and groans incessantly and is generally uncooperative is judged ill-mannered and can be penalized at the discretion of the HSM or trainer. We know one HSM who tired of her competitor's behavior and hitched up the trailer, loaded the pony, and drove off — without saying a word to anyone.

It is also important to consider the relative sizes before mounting a child on a pony. The pair are supposed to present a pleasing picture in the show ring; this can best be accomplished by matching the sizes. Here it is not merely a matter of the height of the pony. A 14-hand pony with a large barrel might be suitable for a large child while a 14-hand pony with a narrow barrel would not. Size is not the only consideration. A trainer will sometimes match an inexperienced rider with a very made, safe animal — which may not be ideal with regard to size, but definitely in regard to manners, i.e. a large made pony and a small inexperienced rider. In this case safety outweighs size considerations.

One must also consider the child's conformation, whether she is short- or long-waisted, short- or long-legged, bulky or slim. Selecting the proper mount for the child affects our perspective of the child and vice versa. Take a pony with a longish back; putting a small child on it draws attention to the length of the back. Similarly, putting a large child on a pony with a short back can emphasize the shortness. Mounting a child with short legs on a pony with a big barrel makes the child's legs look even shorter.

The temperament of the pony must also be suitable for the termpament of the rider; a timid rider is not a good match for an aggressive pony. A quieter mount might be more suitable.

How to Watch A Hunter Seat Class on the Flat (often called "the hack")

In under saddle classes exhibitors show their ponies on the flat. The HSM wants to know what the judge is looking at in an under saddle class. What makes the winning difference? According to AHSA specifications, hunter ponies are to be shown at a walk, trot and canter both ways of the ring. The rider should have light contact with the pony's mouth. The pony should be obedient, alert, responsive, and move freely. Riders may be asked to hand gallop, together, one way of the ring. But no more than eight will be asked to gallop at one time. Ponies are not to gallop in green pony classes.

Gate-keepers and gait-keepers — Gate-keepers are those individuals at the in- and out-gates who try to keep the class moving at a steady pace by getting exhibitors into the ring in a timely manner. You can recognize them by their threats, as in, "If I don't have a large pony on course in ten seconds I'm gong to start calling numbers."

Gait-keepers are riders, one of whose jobs is to ensure that the animal is moving at the proper gait. The *walk* is a four-beat gait; in a hunter division the pony should move with a long, freely moving stride. A good pace must be estabished even at the walk.

The *trot* is a two-beat gait which occurs when the animal moves from one pair of diagonal legs to the other pair. There are three speeds: the sitting trot is slow, the posting trot is faster, while the extended trot matches a longer stride with the speed of the posting trot.

Fences

The HSM also has three speeds: fast (when there are only two classes before the model class), faster (when the model class has been called), and fastest (when the children are entering the ring, ponies in hand, and her competitor has just left the barn).

The *canter* is a three-beat gait; one hind foot strikes the ground first, followed by two diagonal feet and one front foot. A pony is on the *correct lead* when it is cantering to the left with the left front leg leading or when it is cantering to the right with the right front leg leading.

The *hand gallop* is a controlled four-beat gait in which one hind foot strikes, followed by the other hind foot, the diagonal front foot, and the remaining front foot. The hand gallop must be restrained; too quick a pace is penalized for demonstrating a lack of control.

The animals are worked both ways of the ring because some ponies, like humans, can be either right-handed or left-handed and, therefore, can go better in one direction than the other. The gaits must be consistent in that the animal maintains a steady pace. Watch for cantering ponies speeding up on the long sides of the ring or ponies who poke along at the walk.

Obedience and responsiveness — Hunter ponies must respond correctly and quickly to the rider's signals. If a pony *breaks gait*, it is not obedient. This occurs, say, when it is traveling in one gait and breaks to a different gait before asked to do so. The pony must not only obey the rider's commands, but it must do so immediately and with no obvious effort. The judge is able to evaluate the pony's obedience and responsiveness by requesting various *transitions*, changes which occur between gaits or within gaits. For instance, when the pony moves from a walk to a trot, it is making a transition between gaits. When it moves from a sitting trot to an extended trot it is making a transition within a gait. Whether these transitions are performed smoothly and timely is a measure of the animal's responsiveness, which is a function of both its training and the rider's capabilities. The rider's signals must be clear and definite; she must ensure that the pony remains alert. If the pony is not alert at a walk (i.e. the rider is making no demands, so it is not in a listening mode), and is asked to canter, the response might be delays.

The HSM is, of course, always alert.

All of the transitions must be performed smoothly, correctly, immediately, and without obvious effort on the part of the rider and pony. Consider a *downward transition* (moving to a slower gait) from a canter to a walk. When the rider asks for the walk, the pony should come down to it quickly and smoothly. The rider shouldn't have to jerk on the reins and, when she increases her contact with the bit, the pony should respond gracefully — without pinning back its ears or getting behind the bit. The

113

"I want her to go third."

The Correct Lead

transition from a hand gallop to a halt is a weak spot; an immediate and smooth transition is a measure of the rider's control over her mount.

Transitions are also the changes the HSM makes between being a martinet and having her martini (the smoothness of the transition is a function of the number of the latter).

Contact with the horse's mouth — To the judge in a hunter under saddle class, this translates into the fact that the pony is *on the bit*, i.e. it accepts contact without any resistance. Imagine a vertical line descending from the pony's poll to the ground. When the pony is overflexed, its head is held somewhere between the chest and the vertical ine, *behind the vertical*. When this occurs the pony is said to be *behind the bit*. It is *above the bit* when the head is held ahead of the vertical; the nose will be stretched out ahead of the pony in an ungainly fashion and it will look *strung out*. Typically, when a pony is strung out the reins are very loose. If the pony is on the bit then the rider has contact, can ask for changes in pace or direction, and balance the pony (by lightening the forehand).

To the HSM, contact with the horse's mouth translates into a bite; this is to be avoided.

Frame — The way that the pony carries itself is called the *frame*. Judges look for ponies that are collected in that they travel on the bit with their hocks fully engaged. This is called a *balanced frame*. Why is this important? Ponies are taught to respond to both leg and hand signals in specific ways. For instance, they are taught to stop when the rider closes her legs, sits down into the saddle, and fixes her hands. *Fixing the hands* (so that they no longer *give*) holds the forehand back, while *closing the legs* (increasing the pressure) drives the pony into the bit. If the pony is not traveling in the correct frame, then the rider has either lost contact with the hindquarters or the forehand, or both.

For the HSM, traveling in the correct frame, or in a balanced frame, has to do less with physical characteristics and more with state of mind.

Way of going — According to the AHSA, this refers to the way that the animal moves. A pony is called a *good mover* if it moves freely from the shoulder, with a minimal amount of knee action. The legs move close to the ground, with the feet seeming to skim it, covering a large distance. If you watch a good mover traveling, you will notice that its stride is very long and smooth and it almost seems to be floating along the ground; its energy moves the legs forward rather than up and down. A good mover also travels in a straight line along the straight lines; if you look from the front or the back, the legs should appear to move in a straight line.

For the HSM, the way of going refers to how one gets to the show grounds and avoids the temptation to try short-cuts.

Bending and balancing — Ponies exhibited in hunter under saddle classes should travel straight along the straight lines of the ring and bend in the direction of travel along the corners of the ring If a pony doesn doesn't bend correctly in the corners, its balance is compromised.

Showmanship — In a hunter under saddle class, half the battle is having a well-trained mount which is a good mover; after all, it is the animal which is being judged. However, the rest depends on how the animal is shown by the rider.

For instance, no matter how good the pony is, it must be seen by the judge. Unlike the over fences classes, the exhibitors compete in a group — often a very large group. Riders are, therefore, instructed before they enter the ring, to *find a hole*, i.e. a spot on the rail by themselves. If a competitor is boxed in by other riders not only will it be harder to be seen by the judge but it will also be more difficult to make smooth transitions.

Riders must also make some *good passes* in front of the judge. This means passing so that the rider and pony can be seen when they both look good without being obvious. The rider should make a pass when the pony is moving well. If the canter on the left lead is choppy, hide in the crowd; if the trot is particularly nice, let the judge see it. Judges can only penalize or reward what they see. This means that the rider must be aware, not only of where the other riders are (so that she can find a hole or hide herself) but also where a judge is located. Judges can, and often do, move around. If a rider is not aware of the location of other riders in the ring she might get *cut off* or she might do the same to another rider. A rider is cut off when another rider moves in front of her, causing her pony to break gait in order to avoid collisoin.

An HSM can be cut off by a child who doesn't want her advice, by a trainer who doesn't want her interference, or by another HSM who remembers that one of them has to drive home.

How to Watch Pony Hunter Conformation Classes

In the pony hunter division conformation classes are judged first on performance and soundness and then on conformation. After the performance section is completed the judge lines up the class in the order of the ribbons. The ponies are then judged on conformation and the order can be changed. This does happen. Recently one of our ponies pinned first in a small-medium pony hunter class only to be moved back to second on conformation. Moaning about it after to a trainer (it absolutely kills you when this happens to your child and pony), the mother was confronted with a shrug and a rhetorical question, "You want the pony to get a nose job?" Meanwhile, we have been told that its reputation will eventually outweigh its head. We'll see.

116

Ponies are not judged on performance in a model class. First they are judged while standing in a line, head to tail. Then they are jogged and the judge lines up the class in the order of the pinning.

According to the AHSA, conformation refers to quality, substance and soundness. Judges can penalize ponies for structural faults, defects and blemishes in areas which may impair their activity and durability.

The ratio of a pony's body parts, i.e. its proportions, is judged in conformation classes. This refers to, say, the length of the neck, the size of the hindquarters, and the length of the back in relation to the entire animal. Ideally the back is one-third the length of the body (from the chest to the rear end); any deviation is a conformation fault. A long back is penalized because it can lead to weakness. A neck that is too short is penalized because it makes it more difficult for the pony to maintain its balance when jumping. In sum judges penalize proportion faults that either contribute to poor performance or unsound conditions.

Judges look at the angles of the joints, noticing the slope of the shoulder and the angle of the hip. The shoulder should be long and sloping (not too steep an angle) and the hip angle should be at about 90 degrees. Too narrow an angle leads to a short-strided animal and too wide an angle puts pressure on the legs (and can eventually lead to an unsound condition). Judges also notice the angle of the pastern and hoof, ideally 50 degrees in the front and 55 degrees in the hind. This affects the length of stride and the pressure on the foot and legs which, again, can lead to an unsound condition. The judges examine the angles of the joints and penalize those angles which can cause unsound conditions or restrict the animal's range of movement.

Judges penalize physical defects, whether inherited by the pony or resulting from injury. Those defects that can lead to unsound conditions or performance faults are penalized more than defects which are merely unsightly. Thus, a superficial scar would carry less of a penalty than an injury which involved muscle or skeletal damage. Finally, the judges notice whether a pony has lameness, respiratory problems, or blindness.

The HSM may find these classes the most difficult to watch intelligently because a knowledge of conformation faults is highly specialized. Furthermore, the HSM standing at some distance from the ponies cannot see many of the flaws noticed by the judge at close range.

Rather than be discouraged, the HSM can watch the other competitors, noticing what they do to make their ponies look better. Few ponies have perfect conformation, and if one did, you couldn't afford it (or so we were told during a pre-purchase exam). It is fascinating to watch children try to accentuate their ponies' good points while trying to hide the faults.

The HSM may see a child stretching a pony's neck down and out; this creates the look desired in hunter ponies. She may wonder why some pony's tails are braided in mud knots when there is no mud; it is because the

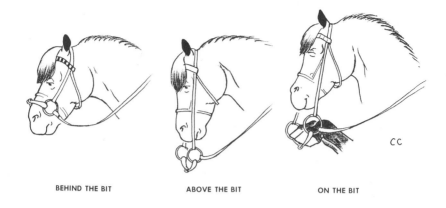

BEHIND THE BIT   ABOVE THE BIT   ON THE BIT

Pony . . . Rider . . . Judge . . . Trainer

hindquarters are well-proportioned and a braided mud knot draws attention to them. A mud knot can also disguise a thin and wispy tail. A loose, flowing tail, on the other hand, disguises poor hindquarters. If the neck is too short, an uninterrupted line of tiny braids visually lengthens it.

The HSM may notice competitors tapping their ponies on the muzzle with a crop, to keep them from moving forward, or crumple up some cellophane (usually from a cigarette pack) to get the pony's attention. She wants it to look alert, with the ears forward.

The HSM will find that in any conformation classes presentation of the pony can decide the winners as much as the actual conformation. She will hear that a chid *stood that pony up well.* Knowing this, she can observe not only the ponies, but also the children who model them.

How to Watch a Hunter Seat Equitation Class on the Flat or "Not to Jump" (As the Rule Book Has It)

Equitation is the act or art of riding on horseback. In an equitation class only the rider is being judged; so, given that her mount can perform the required class routine and is under sufficient control, you can concentrate on watching your child. In order to understand how the class is pinned, you must also watch the other riders, not just the one who is making your stomach roll with nervousness.

> Anna Jane White-Mullins says *(Juding Hunters and Hunters Seat Equitation)* that although equitation riders don't need the fanciest mount to get a ribbon, they do need something that doesn't have severe locomotion, conformation, or disposition problems which put the rider at a disadvantage.
>
> The worst faults in an equitation class are those which show that the rider is not in control: a runaway pony, bucking, rearing, and kicking at other ponies. These are dangerous and therefore penalized the most severely.

It should be noted that judges may eliminate competitors who do not conform, so be sure that your child's personal appointments, i.e. her jacket, hat, breeches, spurs, etc., are appropriate and that her tack falls under the AHSA guidelines which permit regulation snaffles, pelhams, and full bridles, all with cavesson nose bands. Judges may penalize a pony with non-conventional bits or nose bands. Boots and conservative colored bandages are allowed. The saddle type is not specified and martingales are permitted in classes over jumps and in clsses requiring both jumping and hacking. Otherwise, martingales are not allowed.

And now the child is in the ring, properly attired and mounted. How do you watch intelligently? What do you look for? What is good, and bad, and very bad? Your child's riding consists of two parts: her overall body position during the different gaits and her ability to make the pony perform. We often hear complaints (especially from the rider) that the judge shouldn't have considered some fault because it was the pony's mistake, not the rider's, and that in an equitation class only the rider is supposed to be judged. In fact, one cannot disregard the pony because the rider is responsible for how it goes.

The AHSA Rule Book in Article 2108 lays down guidelines:

Seat and hands:
1. *General.* Rider should have a workmanlike appearance, seat and hands light and supple, conveying the impression of complete control should any emergency arise.

A workmanlike appearance implies a look of concentration and seriousness about the performance on the child's face; the rider appears ready to cope with any problem.

2. *Hands.* Hands should be over and in front of the horse's withers, knuckles thirty degrees inside the vertical, hands slightly apart and making a straight line from horse's mouth to rider's elbow. Method of holding reins optional and bight of reins may fall on either side. However, all reins must be picked up at the same time.

The proper position of the hands is not decided arbitrarily; it reflects the best position for the rider to maintain effective control and influence over her mount. Watch the other riders and notice that the hands are light and supple. The good riders will have their fingers closed on the reins; they will *not:*

Be pulling on the reins or hanging on the horse's mouth for suport; *watch for* a rider behind the motion.

Use the reins for balance; *watch for* the rider leaning slightly forward, on the reins (often the hands are carried low).

Be severe; *watch for* the pony reacting abruptly.

Be passive; *watch* for the pony traveling with its head poking way out and its weight more on its forelegs.

Be holding the reins too far in front of the pony's withers; *watch for* the rider's body angled too far forward.

Be held behind the withers; *watch for* too long reins, with hands held at the stomach when halting.

Be rigid; *watch for* arms which don't follow the motion of the pony's head (though, in fact, this is very little motion — rider's hands should not appear to move very much).

Be carried too high.

Be flat; *watch for* hands that look like puppy paws or piano hands.

Have elbows flapping in the breeze; *watch for* chicken wings.

You may try to watch the hands of the HSM. You will note that they are never still — from hand-waving to hand-wringing to hand-clapping.

Choose a pony "that does not have severe locomotion problems"

Sign up lines

3. *Basic Position.* The eyes should be up and shoulders back. Toes should be at an angle suited to rider's conformation, ankles flexed in, heels down, calf of leg in contact with horse and slightly behind girth. Iron should be on the ball of the foot and must not be tied to the girth.

First the eyes. They shoud be up — a simple enough command, but difficult to execute. There is a strong temptation for a rider to look down, especially an inexperienced one. One might want to check diagonals (at a trot), check leads (at a canter), make sure that the hands are correctly placed, look at the pony to make sure that it halts when asked, see if it is bending on a turn, or look at a jump (both approaching and over it). And if you have ever ridden you know that there are numerous other reasons to look down, as in, "Oh my, it's a long way down to fall!"

But the eyes must be up. If a rider needs to check diagonals or leads it should be with a soft, quick, downward glance. It is much better for a rider to learn to feel whether the pony is correct when bending, halting, etc.

As well as being up, the eyes should be looking ahead to where the rider wishes the pony to go — but not so far that her head gets out of line with the rest of the body. She should not, for example, be turning her head so far that she is almost looking over her shoulder. She must look ahead enough, only turning slightly to anticipate bends around corners. On a straight line the rider's eyes (and face) should be straight ahead.

Where the rider looks is where she goes (and she does not want to go down), her body following instinctively where her eyes direct it. The rider looking up at a halt will have a pony performing a neater, more balanced movement. And over fences the body and pony will follow the eye. If a rider stares down a fence there is a much greater chance that her body will follow her eye down and her pony will end up chipping in instead of moving forward.

The eyes, as well as charting the forward movement of the rider and mount, will also be working peripherally, taking in ponies moving up on her and causing trouble. She will use her eyes to avoid congestion and spot open places to show off.

For the rest of the basic position we shall start with the leg and move up, because if the leg position is incorrect it will cause problems in position for the rest of the body.

The basic position of the HSM should be as relaxed as possible. Take a deep breath and lower your shoulders. Tell yourself that the most important things are enjoyment and safety.

Feet and Legs

The toes should be at an angle best suited to the rider's conformation. The angle of the toe should be slightly turned out, away from the pony while bringing the calf against its side. The ankle *flexed in* means that the

122

ankle should be bent slightly towards the pony's side. A small part of the sole of the boot is visible to the spectator if the ankle is bent correctly.

Heels down is something most people have heard about riding. The heel comes down when the rider lets her weight sink into her heels.

The *calf of the leg in contact with horse* means that the side of the rider's leg is against the side of the pony (an important means of communication). The breaking of the ankle helps to keep the calf on the pony. The HSM can watch from the side to see daylight between the saddle and the leg. If she can, the calf is not gainst the pony.

The *knee* should rest against the saddle. This may be impossible for a long-legged rider on a narrow pony. Then, in order to keep the calf on the pony, the rider may have to take her knee off the saddle — an example of the unsuitability of pony and rider. It is most important, though, that the calf be on the pony, so it is a lesser fault for the knee to come away from the saddle than for the calf to come off the side.

The *legs slightly behind girth* means that the rider's legs are not too far forward or too far back. They should be steady, not move very much — certainly not swing back and forth. It is a greater fault for the legs to be too far forward than too far behind the girth because the upper body falls behind the motion and causes the rider to hang on the pony's mouth for balance.

Overall, the position of the feet and legs should make the rider secure. She should be able to negotiate uneven terrain at various gaits and jump appropriately sized obstacles without losing her balance. The HSM can correct mistakes in foot and leg position and make sure that the rider is sitting in the center of her pony and not leaning to one side — that she is, in fact, secure.

Security for the HSM has little to do with leg position, everything to do with having a good map, a good pony, a good trainer, a good motel and a good friend with whom to share pre-class jitters.

Upper Body

Overall, the upper body should be straight, with the neck and head part of a continuing line from the waist through the back. The neck and head should not be stuck out, nor should the head be cocked to one side. Even the chin should be tucked in rather than jutting out. Instructors often tell riders to feel a string pulling their bodies up from the saddle through the top of their heads.

The *back* should not be rounded nor should it be hollow. The rounded or *roached* back is often accompanied by rounded shoulders. The hollow back often is accompanied by buttocks pushed out and shoulders forced back unnaturally. The former is a more serious fault than the latter.

The upper body should not be *ahead of the motion*, i.e. too far forward. This is often caused by legs too far behind the girth and results in a rider

Lines of spectators

Lines looking at Pony Final results

leaning on her hands or the pony's neck. Nor should the upper body be *behind the motion*, i.e. leaning behind the vertical (the 90 degree angle formed by the rider's body and the saddle). This is often accompanied by legs too far forward and results in the rider supporting herself by pulling on the reins and the pony's mouth.

Finally, the rider's upper body should not be thrown back and forth by the movement of the pony.

The good HSM is not thrown back and forth either. Her position of patience and good humor remains constant despite the sometimes erratic pace of child, trainer, and show.

> 4. *Position in Motion.* At the Walk and Slow Trot body should be vertical; Posting Trot inclined forward; Canter half way between the Posting Trot and the Walk. Galloping and Jumping same inclination as the Posting Trot.

At a *walk* you should see that the rider's thighs and buttocks go with the movement of the pony naturally, not in a forced manner. There should be rhythm and forward impulsion, i.e. onward tendency. The pony should be using itself, pushing forward with its hind legs underneath.

At a *sitting trot* the rider should not bounce out of the saddle. Her back should remain tight, her upper body stretched tall, absorbing the bounce with a relaxed seat rather than a relaxed back. She may collect her pony to make the trot easier to sit, but she must make sure that the trot still has rhythm and forward impulsion. The angle of the pelvis is just a few degrees in front of the vertical. Again, the upper body should not be too far forward or behind the vertical.

At a *posting trot* the rider's body should be inclined forard at about a 20 degree angle, no more. She should be posting on her thighs and crotch rather than the buttocks, only touching the saddle lightly when she comes down. The cadence of the posting should be maintained and the movement up and forwad should be balanced with the rider not needing her hands for support. She must post on the correct diagnonal.

At a *canter* the upper body of the rider will be the same as it was at the walk and sitting trot, only a few degrees in front of the vertical. The rider sits deep in the saddle, her bottom relaxed and her thighs and buttocks absorbing the movement of the pony. She is no longer on her crotch. And she will be one with the saddle, not sliding back and forth with the pony's stride. The pony must be on the correct lead.

> 5. *Mounting and Dismounting.* To mount, take up reins in left hand and place hand on withers. Grasp stirrup leather with right hand and insert left foot in stirrup and mount. To dismount, rider may either step down or slide down. The size of rider must be taken into consideration.

One of the 18 tests which the judge may ask the riders to perform is to dismount and mount. If riders are asked to change horses, they would also be expected to do it correctly.

More Horse Show Math
(Horse Show Geometry — Or How To Figure Angles)

The ankle angle — Formed by the foot and lower leg.

The open angle — The angle of the hip on the approach to the fence.

The HSM's angle (or perspective) — Which is often different from the judge's.

Closing the angle — When the rider's body goes forward over a fence, letting the pony's take-off close the angle.

The knee angle — Formed by the thigh and the calf.

The angling of by the child — To get a new pony, rent a golf cart, or have yet another doughnut.

Angles in front of the vertical — 10 degrees at a walk, 20 degrees at a posting trot, etc.

The hip angle — Formed by the thigh and upper body.

The angling that the HSF doesn't get to do anymore — Horse shows being substituted for fishing trips.

The elbow angle — Formed by the lower and upper arm.

The angling by the trainer — To take the child and pony on the Florida circuit.

In general remember that the particulars of leg, hand, and upper body position apply to every gait; they remain correct not only when the pony is moving, but also when it is standing, i.e. during the line-up.

The Ability to Make the Pony Perform

Performance is what the rider is able to make her pony do. She must keep it moving forward at all gaits, maintain an even tempo, and keep it alert and out of trouble in the ring.

Performance for the HSM is what she is able to make her child do — go to bed on time, smile though her heart is breaking, be polite, eat at least some protein, vegetables and fruit, and keep her riding clothes relatively clean. That kind of thing.

The pony should move forward with a definite rhythm in all gaits, including the walk. It should be *collected*, or in a shorter frame in which its impulsion comes from the hindquarters. Collection is achieved by putting the animal on the bit, using leg pressure (from the calf) and *half halts*. The legs drive the pony forward into the bit; the hands, which then do half halts, keep it from moving faster.

Collection is an important concept for the HSM to master as well. Before the show there is the collection of the tack and clothes. At the show there is the collection of her wits and her child's bits and pieces, as in, "Who

126

saw my jodhpur straps? I go second in the next class." At the end of the show there is the collection of all the same tack and clothes with the addition of ribbons and checks. And then there is the collection that the show management is interested in, as in, "Oh, Mom, did you go to the tack shop and show office yet? I charged some bit keepers and added an equitation class."

The rider is penalized if her pony is *behind the bit* (has its nose too close to its chest) *pulling* (dragging on the rider's hands and keeping its weight on its forehand), or *above the bit* (holding its head in the air).

The rider should be able to *bend* the pony around turns. The animal will appear to be molded around the rider's inside leg, the degree of the bend proportionate to the turn, and the whole body of the pony, from head to tail, describing an arc that follows the turn.

Overheard — Trainer to child: "What were you thinking about on that turn, your boyfriend?"

The rider should be able to get her pony to make smooth transitions, both upward and downward. When she asks for a canter the pony should canter, not trot faster and faster until it breaks into a canter. In a downward transition slower transition looks better than an abrupt slowdown.

And, finally, it isn't necessarily the famous pony that wins. The hard-working equitation rider can turn in blue ribbon rounds on a mediocre pony.

More horse show geometry — Lines also play an important role in horse shows:

Lines from the rider's elbow to the pony's mouth.

The lines on our faces from worry and laughter.

Lines on which jumps are placed.

The lines at the wash stall and washroom.

Parallel lines formed by the rider's and pony's backs over fences.

The lines at the registration trailer and the concession stand.

Straight lines, i.e. imaginary lines through the head, shoulder, hip, and heel of the rider (if her position is correct).

The lines of filled parking spaces when you arrive at the show.

Line-ups, i.e. the lines formed by ponies to find out who pinned.

The lines your child gives you about why she didn't pin.

Broken lines.

The lines you were supposed to print your address on and instead you wrote down the pony's name.

The straight line of a pony's leg in a conformation class.

. . . and then there are circles:

Practice circles.

The circles you can go in trying to get the pony's measurement card.

Courtesy circles.

Circles kids make in order to find a clear spot on the rail.

Equitation tests — The AHSA has established a series of tests which let the rider know, at each level of competition, what might be expected of her. Thus, if the description of an equitation class advises that Tests 1 to 6 may be used, the competitor is forewarned that she might be asked to perform these tests in the class (and want to practice them before the show). Judges may choose to test only some of the riders in a given class. These tests can be found in the AHSA Rule Book Article 2113:

Halt (4 to 6 seconds) — and back.

Hand Gallop

Figure eight at trot, demonstrating change of diagonals. At left diagonal, rider should be sitting the saddle when left front leg is on the ground; at right diagonal, rider should be sitting the saddle when right front leg is on the ground; when circling clockwise at a trot, rider should be on left diagonal; and when circling counter-clockwise, rider should be on right diagonal.

Figure eight at canter on correct lead, demonstrating simple change of lead (whereby the horse is brought back into a walk or trot and re-started into a canter on the opposite lead). Figures to be commenced in center of two circles so that one change of lead is shown.

Work collectively at a walk, trot, or canter.

Pull up and halt (4 to 6 seconds).

Jump fences on figure 8 course.

Ride without stirrups or drop and pick up stirrups.

Jump low fences at a walk and trot as well as a canter. The maximum height for a walk fence is 3'. The maximum height and spread for a trotting fence is 3'.

10. Dismount and mount.

11. Turn on the forehand.

12. Figure 8 at canter on correct lead, demonstrating flying change of lead.

13. Execute serpentine at a trot and canter on correct lead, demonstrating simple or flying changes of lead.

14. Change leads on a line, demonstrating a simple or flying change of lead.

15. Change horses, the equivalent of two tests.

16. Canter on counter lead, with no more than 12 horses at one time.

17. Turn on the haunches.

18. Demonstration ride of approximately one minute. Rider must advise judge beforehand which ride she plans to demonstrate.

Collapsing on landing

Ultimate case of "getting left"!

George Morris has an excellent discussion of these equitation tests in his book, *Hunter Seat Equitation* (Doubleday).

How To Watch Hunter Seat Equitation Over Fences or How To Quiet Your Terror By Becoming Intellectually Involved

Once the HSM has learned to watch equitation on the flat she is more than half way to watching it over fences. Only a fraction of the time that the rider is in the ring doing the course is actually spent over fences. Consequently, the HSM can apply much of her knowledge of judging on the flat.

She will remember to watch the lower leg position: toe out, ankle flexed, calf on, knee on, and leg unmoving. This position is correct over fences as well.

She will notice the upper body. It should be in a straight line from the base of the spine to the top of the head, whatever its angle in front of the vertical. Over fences this angle is closed, with the rider's back approximately parallel to the pony's. Rounded backs and shoulders, hollow backs, shoulders rigidly held back, and backs that swing back and forth excessively are faults over fences as well as on the flat.

She will note whether the eyes are looking ahead.

And she will watch for hand faults: hands held too high (a rider too far out of the saddle); hands held too low (a rider too far forward); and hands which do not *give* over a fence (a rider who gets left and then catches the pony in the mouth). She will watch for the rider who is stiff and tense and consequently has *set hands*. She can see a result of set hands in a pony's open mouth during a jump that is flat because the pony cannot stretch out its neck and head. She can watch for hands that lose contact with the pony's mouth, with the reins looping or going slack at the fence; hands that fiddle the last few strides before a fence when the pony needs to be left alone to concentrate on the jump; and hands that are flat, knuckles up, causing the rider's elbows to flap.

Faults on the Approach, Over Fence, and Landing

Getting left — The rider's upper body position in the air is behind the motion of the pony. On the approach the rider's legs are probably too far forward, or the pony jumped before the rider expected it.

There is also the girth which gets left, and the jodhpur straps which get left, and the choker which gets left, and the . . .

Jackknife — This occurs when a rider has a position over the fence of straight legs, probably too far forward, with little or no bend in the knee

All shapes and sizes

and hip. It causes an excessive bend at the waist with the rider thrust too far forward, balancing over the pony's neck. A rounded back often accompanies this position on the approach as well as over the fence. The rider's weight on the pony's forehand makes it difficult for the pony to jump.

Jumping up on the pony's neck — On the approach the rider stays too close to the vertical with the upper body and then at the fence must make a big move to catch up to the pony's forward thrust.

Ducking — The rider drops her head below one side of the pony's crest while over the fence.

HSMs also duck from time to time, as in ducking out of barn work or ducking out of driving the kids to the barn at 5:30 in the morning to braid.

Dropping the head and looking down — If the rider drops her head and looks down, her balance is affected; this, in turn, compromises the pony's balance and can lead to a bad fence.

Perching — This results from legs too far back and upper body too far forward, ahead of the pony's motion on the approach. It will sometimes cause refusals because of the extra weight on the pony's forehand and the inability of the legs to drive forward from this position. It is also a tenuous position for the rider because, if there is a refusal, she is likely to be pitched forward and off. If the pony does not refuse, the perching can still cause rubs with the pony's forelegs hanging because of the forward weight.

Not enough release and fixed hands — The pony's balance in the air is inhibited by not being able to stretch its neck and head. It will jump flat in order not to be hit in the mouth by the bit.

This fault is also used by the trainer to describe the over-protective HSM.

Dropping back too soon — The rider's seat comes down on the pony's back, hitting the saddle before the pony has landed completely. It usually happens to riders whose legs are too far forward and who are behind the motion.

Collapsing on landing — The rider's upper body pivots forward as the pony lands because of lack of balance, usually because the leg is not strong enough; perhaps there is too much knee and thigh contact and not enough calf.

An HSM can be said to collapse on landing when she gets home, before she does the laundry and washes out the cooler.

Leaning — This causes the redistribution of the rider's weight and can make a pony jump crooked. Leaning can be caused by a head cocked to one side, or by a rider looking back at the last fence. Leaning causes a loss of position and security for the rider, and may make a pony jump badly, hang a leg, etc.

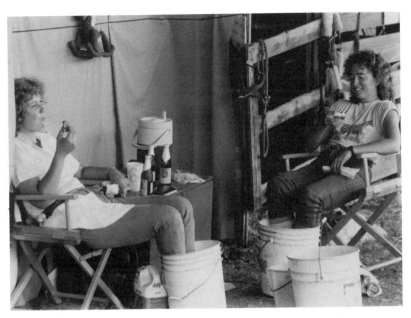

Grooms "collapsing on landing," in chairs at last, after the show

'SHOW HOW'

PERSONAL

"GET THE BLUES"

HORSESHOW SUPPORT
FOR
CHILDREN OR ADULTS

LEARN WINNING WAYS

ENGLISH OR WESTERN
EXPERIENCED "SHOWMOM" FOR HIRE
WILL TRAVEL WITH YOU TO SHOWS TO
HELP WITH EVERYTHING - TEACH YOU
THE "INS & OUTS"- FROM WHAT TO TAKE,
TO LOADING FOR HOME & SURVIVE IT!

CALL SUE - HERNDON, VA. 703-435-9156

The future is yours . . . the HSM as career woman

133

Understandably, some HSMs lean in favor of their own children, as in, "My Dottie should have had that class."

Overall Performance

The rider should enter the ring confidently, making the entry circle large enough to establish the pace and stride necessary to do the course evenly. It is within this circle that she should make adjustments rather than on course. The first quarter of the circle should be a posting trot — followed by a few beats of sitting trot, and thence to the canter and the two-point position until, by the end of the circle, she has established the pace needed for the course.

At the end of the course another circle is made, maintaining the same pace and moving from canter to walk in a smooth transition.

Overheard— HSM to HSM: "I've always felt somehow that there ought to be 9 fences with the judge counting the best 8."

On course, the competitor should ride out her lines, keeping them straight and not cutting corners, being careful to bend on the turns. According to George Morris (p. 118, *Hunter Seat Equitation*), the equitation rider maintains two-point contact on straight lines and three-point position on the turns. A rider is in two-point contact when she shifts her weight from her seat to her legs; her seat is out of the saddle. In three-point position the rider's seat is deep in the saddle with her legs on the pony.

The rider should maintain the pace she set in the beginning throughout the course. The pony should not break from the canter or refuse a fence. It should be on the bit and, overall, the performance should be done smoothly and with apparent ease. The expression on the rider's face should be serious, i.e. workmanlike concentration.

Overheard — Trainer to rider: "And take it easy. I could fall over those fences gracefully."

The rider is responsible for seeing that the pony is on the correct lead throughout the course. It is equally correct to land on the right lead for the next fence or do a flying lead change at the beginning of a turn (although, for advanced work, one might prefer to land on the correct lead). Courses are set up with necessary lead changes as part of the test.

The rider is responsible for finding a good take-off spot for the pony. Bad spots are easily seen, with the pony taking off too far away from the jump or chipping in at the fence. The HSM can watch the rider's ability to make adjustments between the fences, increasing the length of the stride or collecting the pony and steadying it in order to reach the right spot. It is important that the rider try to do this; the more subtly it is accomplished, the higher she will be rated.

134

The good HSM should be able to make adjustments: collecting her wits when too many people ask her too many questions at the same time, and steadying her nerves and her impatience without screaming (even though it is a five-hour drive home.

HSM Equitation or The Art of Being a Horse Show Mother

An HSM does *not:*
Let on how much she would like her child to be champion, even to herself.

Display any outward signs of pleasure when a competitor makes a mistake in the ring.

Rush to the instructor as soon as her child completes a course over fences, wanting to know how the round went; the trainer may have other students to observe in that class.

Suggest changes in either tack or performance just before the child enters the ring; she saves them for the next competition.

Yell instructions from the sideline.

Disagree with the trainer, at least not in public.

Criticize a performance when her knowledge is minimal.

Let a competitor be embarrassed by the antics of her non-showing siblings or cousins who came to observe.

An HSM handles herself perfectly in the following situations:
She knows when to congratulate and when to remain silent, accepting that sometimes anything she might do is wrong.

She is friendly and supportive to other HSMs and their kids.

Unlike the competitor, she tries to smile.

She is never in bad form, i.e. never so eccentric as to attract attention and embarrass a child.

She knows when to meet her rider at the out-gate and when to keep her distance. We know an HSM who is not allowed to watch a class, at least where the daughter can see her from the ring.

She never stays out too late relaxing after a strenuous show day. *Overheard* — HSM to HSM: "I knew it was late when I got to the motel and the braiders were leaving."

Trainers have been known to point

5

Afterward

BY AHSA RECKONING, the show season ends on
November 30th. This also marks the last day that a pony can maintain its
green status. In our opinion the HSM also loses her green status on this
day; after a year of showing, no mother can hope for an exemption on the
grounds of inexperience. However, we heard a story about a child who
appeared in the show ring with her jodhpurs tucked into her paddock
boots because she lost her straps. She had been showing more than a year.
Where was her mother?

This is the time to evaluate the past season's activities and make plans
for the coming year. Here are some things you need to think about.

Pony Performance

How did the pony perform this past year? What are its capabilities and
limitations? Are its abilities compatible with your goals? Is it the right one
to go on with? You need to think about what divisions your child plans to
compete in next year; a pony that is competitive in the short stirrup
division might not be a winner in the pony hunter division.

An HSM's Guide to Ponies

They come in all colors, shapes, sizes, temperaments, and abilities. We
noticed:

Some ponies are always alert, reacting to the environment.
Some are gentle and accept whatever is done to or asked of them.
Some stay clean; others find the smallest dropping to roll in
Some are experienced; the question is whether they are experienced at
winning.

Some get *up* at shows and need to be lunged or turned out before competition.

Some will not measure as ponies, so make the measurement card a condition of purchase.

Some are easy-going; others are brats . . . they bite and kick.

Some are affectionate; others seem oblivious to such gestures.

Some are aggressive; others are lazy.

It is worth the effort to find a pony which is compatible with your child in terms of size, temperament, and ability as well as the child's goals. Often compromises have to be made; the HSM may find herself juggling the child's goals, family fortune, and personal sentiments. The last is no small matter — ponies have a way of wriggling into the hearts of children and mothers.

Here are some suggestions for the HSM. If you own a mount which is not competitive in the pony hunter division, consider pony jumper classes. If it is not competitive at *A* shows, consider *B* or *C* shows, or even unrated local shows; sometimes local competitions can be the most fun for children. Or, you might pick and choose the divisions entered at shows. One child at our barn will be showing a medium pony in the pony hunter division (in which the two of them will be competitive), but not in the equitation classes (in which a size disparity puts them at a disadvantage). The HSM should remember that just as there is not a perfect child, there is not a perfect pony to match. But at least ponies are subject to pre-purchase examination.

An HSM's Guide to Buying and Leasing Ponies

It is our observation that although the HSM might not know a great deal about ponies and the horse show world, she can remedy this to a great extent by knowing the right questions to ask. Nowhere is this truer than when buying or leasing a pony. Here are some things that every HSM should think about and ask beforehand:

1. How does buying differ from leasing? Ponies, like houses, can be either purchased or leased. When you purchase one it's yours, for better or worse. Leasing is like renting in that you pay an agreed-upon sum for the use of the pony for an agreed-upon length of time. When that time expires, you return it to the owner.

2. How does your child feel about leasing versus owning a pony? Sometimes it is more fun to show an animal that you own; on the other hand, leasing can be a means for your child to show a pony that you could not otherwise afford. An experienced pony leased for a short time is not only less expensive, but it also teaches a child new things, gives her confidence, and helps to improve her riding skills. However, sometimes leasing a made pony that has been a consistent winner can put pressure on

Horse Show Kids have been known to learn by example

a child; she might feel that she has to win. Or she might think that since you are paying for the pony you expect certain things, like blue ribbons, in return. It is important for the HSM to remember that any pony takes time to get used to and that made ponies may not be as easy to ride as they appear.

3. Does your child like the pony that you are considering? Or is she intimidated by it?

4. Does the pony have bad habits? Some are famous for things other than their show records. Biting, kicking, and pulling on a lead rope are not fun for a child to contend with. We discovered that asking a rhetorical question at the in-gate in the presence of people who know the pony (usually other HSMs) such as: "Pony dear, don't you ever slow down?", can elicit a helpful response such as, "Only after four shows in a row during the summer." For this reason, if you can, you might take the pony to a show before you make a decision.

5. What is the pony's show record and how recently was it made? Famous ponies that have been out in the pasture or used as brood mares for the past few years may not be in their prime. And when you're told that the pony has done everything, ask for specifics. After all, it is possible that having done everything could include some things you would rather it had not done. And if you're told that it won at the Pony Finals, ask "Won what?" There is a significant difference between winning the model class and winning the jumping class.

6. Find out how it goes in the cold. Some ponies have a great deal more energy in the winter and need to be lunged extensively before a class over fences. It is wise to find out just what showing it in the winter months will entail.

7. Is the pony body-clipped and how does it tolerate clipping? If this is a problem, find out how previous owners coped with it. Did they use tranquilizers? These stay in the bloodstream for three or four days, so think ahead when you are planning to show. Is a twitch sufficient? Or is this a situation in which the same person needs to work with the pony to give it confidence?

8. Always find out whether the pony shows on any medication and if so, what it is, how it is obtained and administered, and how much it costs — assuming that it is legal. Sometimes a powder is cheaper than a paste but harder to get the pony to take. And find out what side effects the medication has — you especially want to be aware of anything that excites or depresses ponies.

More Questions About the Pony

What kind of shoes does it wear? Don't laugh, shoeing is an art and can affect a pony's way of moving, not to mention the HSM's pocketbook.

140

Does it stand to be shod or does it need to be held, or even tranquilizied?

Can it be turned out with other ponies and horses?

How are its stall manners? A pony who won't let a child into the stall can discourage even the bravest of children. And the HSM won't feel good when the barn manager complains about the pony that cribs or weaves.

Does it load easily for trailering?

What kinds of bits have been used by other trainers and riders who worked with the pony?

Are there any suggestions for working with it, especially the first few times?

Mother's Aid

Have your child take a few lessons on a new pony from the trainer who has been working with it. You may pick up a few useful tips. And your child will benefit from working with a trainer who knows the pony's ins and outs.

Does the pony come with a blanket, sheet, or bridle? Since these items are purchased to fit, the previous owner may have no use for them.

What does it eat? Are there acceptable alternatives? (Some feeds are much more expensive than others.) How much does it get fed and how often?

When was it last wormed and with what?

When did it last have shots, what were they, and did it have any adverse reactions?

Does it have a measurement card? Is the card permanent? Can you have it when you pick up the pony?

Is its Coggins up-to-date? And can you have a copy?

Is the pony registered with the AHSA? In whose name is it registered? When you buy it, contact the AHSA to have the registration put in your name.

If you are leasing it, in whose name must the pony be shown?

And finally, the cost. How much? Don't hesitate to ask. Find out whether a cashier's check is required.

If you're leasing, there are special considerations:

Do you pay by the month or all at once for the entire term of the lease?

If you have to return the pony, do you get any of the prepaid lease back?

Under what conditions can you return it? If it becomes unsound, can you return it and get your money refunded? What if your child and the pony just don't get along?

Who pays the vet and farrier bills?

Is the pony insured? Waht does the insurance cover and who pays for it?

Do you have any liability exposure?

Think ahead about all of the things that could go wrong. For instance,

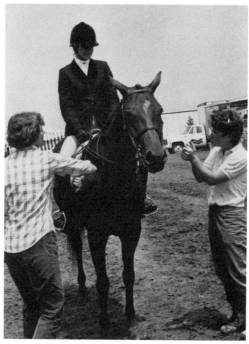

Trainers are always part of the action.

suppose you leased a particular pony because it is qualified for showing and then it is not accepted by a show committee. Would a portion of your lease fee be returned?

Now that you are thoroughly intimidated — terrified may be a better word — relax. It sounds a lot more complicated than it is. But even with professional guidance you still need to ask lots and lots of questions.

An HSM's Guide to Riders

And there are the riders. You need to think about how the child did during the past year. What are her capabilities? Is she an equitation rider or does her strength lie in being an effective rider? What are *her* goals? Should she stay in the pony division or move to a horse? Is her current mount still suitable? The HSM will discover that riders are as varied as ponies.

Some riders are aggressive and cajole their instructors into raising the rail *just one more hole.*

Some are timid, as in, "You want *me* to jump *that?*"

Some are neat, know where every bit of tack is, and that it's clean; others forget something different at every show.

Some have an enormous amount of self-confidence; others don't.

Some have good balance; others fall off a lot.

Some are pretty and do well in equitation classes.

Some are effective and can make the pony look good and do well in performance classes.

Some are self-starters; others need to be motivated, as in, "If that pony isn't bathed and braided by 8 PM, you won't be showing tomorrow."

Some know every ribbon and every point; others can't remember which ribbon came from which class and what happened to the payback check except that they get half of it whenever it turns up.

Some pore over every issue of *The Chronicle of the Horse* and check out equestrian-related materials at the library.

Some aren't interested in theory and prefer to learn through trial-and-error.

Overheard — HSM to HSM: "I don't know what to do. She hides in the washroom so she can miss her classes. Do you think it's time for another sport?"

An HSM's Guide to Trainers

You need to assess your trainer's performance and decide whether to stay with him. Does he work well with your child and animal? Are his goals compatible with yours and your child's? For example, if you want to qualify for the indoor shows it is difficult to stay with a trainer who only wants to attend competitions in the summer months. On the other hand,

In schooling as in life brothers can help sisters get into tight corners - in this case with the trainer's direction

The view of her child most often seen by the HSM

you prefer local shows in a relaxed atmosphere while your trainer wants highly competitive *A* shows. We found that trainers also come in all shapes, sizes, and dispositions:

Some trainers smile a lot.

Some yell a lot.

Some talk constantly during a lesson, and not always to their students.

Some are sarcastic.

Some have philosophies and lesson plans.

Some appear to fly by the seat of their pants, but have a special way with kids and ponies.

Some drop names.

Some have their names dropped.

Some show horses; others get on horses and ponies to school them.

Some are male, some are female; toughness and success do not appear to be sex-linked.

Some use body language.

Some stick to bawdy language.

Some have a sense of humor.

Some are friendly with show families and kids; others more aloof and business-like.

Some are famous; others infamous.

Some have entourages and barns with lovely extras you see in glossy advertisements.

Some operate with volunteers and HSMs.

Most appear helpful and friendly to one another (honor among trainers?).

Out of this no conclusions can readily be drawn, except that with all the variations available, it is important to find a trainer who suits your child and with whom you can get along. Look for someone whose methodology appeals to you and is suitable for your goals. It is worthwihle working hard at getting along with the person you choose. Finally, don't forget that most trainers, like children and HSMs, need recognition and praise. They have responsibilities and worries; indeed, they even have lives away from the barn. They have moods, good days and bad days; so don't take short tempers or distractions personally and help your child do the same.

New Goals

Overheard — HSM to HSM: "I sent one pony to Chicago to be bred, the other to Florida for the winter shows, and my daughter to France for a school trip. I stayed home."

This is a good time to define your goals for the coming year. If you want your child and pony to qualify for the indoor shows, you and your entire family need to have a clear understanding of the time, money, and effort

145

An HSM braiding

Perfect HSM apparel

involved in attending the number of shows necessary to qualify. You must also determine whether it is realistic to expect that your pony can accumulate the number of points required; the competition is tough.

You need to develop early in the year a strategy for showing. *Horse Show Magazine* (published by the AHSA) is very helpful; in the late fall, it publishes a list of the following year's AHSA-recognized shows. This list is updated in subsequent issues. You will decide whether to show primarily in your zone (only points earned in your zone count toward the zone award) or to include shows outside; whether to attend only *A* shows, or include *B* and *C* non-rated shows. Some things to remember: a pony can qualify for the Pony Finals only at an *A* show; the number of points awarded depends on many factors, including the rating of the show, number of competitors, and prize money.

There are other important things to consider when choosing a show: what divisions are offered, who the judge is, and what amenities (such as a pool on the show grounds, shower and toilet facilities, and good food) are available. In our opinion, if we're going to be involved in this, we might as well enjoy ourselves and, all other things being equal, one should choose a show which eases the way.

We learned this the hard way in our first show at a large county fair. We had no idea of the difficulties associated with showing at a fairground. One child went directly from her class over fences to ride the Spaceship Enterprise, only to lose her lunch over her only pair of jodhpurs (to say nothing of the trainer who rode the Spaceship Enterprise, only to . . .) The marching bands warmed up near a pony that had never heard drum-beats; the parking restrictions were never in our favor; and we had unattractive (disgusting) rest room facilities because we came in the fifth day of the fair.

Should you find yourself at a less-than-perfect show, try to make the best of the situation. Follow Dale Carnegie's advice: "If you have a lemon, make lemonade." This was made clear to us at the county fair. We quickly realized that we were part of the livestock exhibit; through our barn there was non-stop traffic of families (complete with children, parents, grandparents, aunts and uncles), little old ladies who exclaimed, "That horse reminds me of the gray mare I had when I was a kid," boy-friends and girl-friends. It turned out that everyone who came to the fair wanted to see the ponies. People casually reached in to pet them, fed them (no one knew what), and even stood outside the stall talking to them.

In fact, it was at another less-than-perfect horse show that this book was conceived. So make the most of every show, make the most of being a Horse Show Mother. Go out and buy those hunting prints for your dining room walls. Needlepoint a pillow with a horsey scene. Tie that scarf (embellished with stirrups and crops) to your handbag. And put on a challis skirt complete with border prints of horses and hounds!

Many hands make light work

At the tack shop at the show

Rider memorizing the course

Isn't there some tack that needs cleaning?

Straight from the Horse's Mouth

Old towels make good rub rags; they make even better ones if they are not put in the dryer (air drying keeps them rough).

Learn to braid; it will save you money.

Borrow our husband's fly fishing vest when you braid. (HSFs don't have time to fish anyway.) You will find that the pockets accomodate yarn, scissors, latch hook, seam ripper, comb, and rubber bands quite nicely.

Make a check-off list of equipment needed for shows, and use it. We photocopy the list so that we don't have to make a new one for each show. If you still forget an important piece of tack, don't worry. Equipment can be borrowed or purchased. Tack shops often set up temporary facilities, in campers, at the show grounds.

Always carry aspirin, bandaids, antacid tablets, etc.; hopefully you won't need them, but somebody always does.

Take riding lessons; you'll appreciate what you are watching, the difficulties of riding, and your child's frustrations and accomplishments.

It sometimes helps to watch your child compete from a distant spot; you can be alone with your terror and hope, as well as other people's comments.

Fly spray, of the equine variety, has been known to get slathered on the desperate HSM; don't expect to smell like Catherine Deneuve. And Mom's suntain lotion works just fine on the pony's muzzle. Use a coconut-scented variety and imagine that you're on the beach.

Ponies are lucky; they're supposed to have wrinkles. When bridling the pony, the bit should not be so tight that the critter is grinning like a used car salesman, or so loose that it clanks against its teeth. A little wrinkle or two at the mouth corners is about right.

Panicky competitors have been known to ask HSMs, "What is the course again?" If you describe the course to the rider, be careful. One child was advised, as she went in the ring, to take the *outhouse* first. The child, having led a comparatively sheltered life, never heard of an outhouse and took the *outside* line (of which the outhouse was not a component) first. "The rider is off course and eliminated," was the prompt response from the judge.

It can be frustrating when the rider forgets the course; a lot of effort goes into getting her into the ring and it's natural for the HSM to get annoyed. One HSM, whose child went off course one too many times, informed the competitor of a new policy: she was to pay the entry fee for each class from which she was eliminated for riding off course. It is reported that she never forgot the course again.

150

An "easy keeper"

Some HSMs favor golf carts for getting around horse shows. There are distinct advantages in this mode of conveyance: your feet don't get wet and muddy; if there is an awning you will stay relatively dry during a rainstorm and when it's not raining the sun won't beat down on you; and riding is less tiring than walking. However, we noticed one HSM, quite slim and trim at the start of the season, who brought her own golf cart to every outdoor show. By the end of the season she was somewhat rotund. There is something to be said for exercise.

It has been said that a rose by any other name would smell as sweet. Although this may also be true of ponies, the HSM should be aware that naming a pony is not to be undertaken lightly. The first thing to be decided is who names the pony — the rider, HSM, breeder, or trainer? A quick glance through the show results posted in *The Chronicle of the Horse* suggests that many small children choose the names for their mounts: Smurfette, Cookie Monster, Garfield, Care Bear, etc. Then there are the ponies which bear the names of their famous parents: Farnley Savoy, Zim's Graduation Day, Woodlands Magic Cloud, Shenandoah Tryfan, Glenmore's Fun Enough, Polaris Starship, etc. Some names must have been chosen for their descriptive value: Who's The Boss, Pocket Change (Is that what was left after the pony was paid for?), Thanks To Daddy, No Reply, and This Is It.

In our opinion, a main consideration in naming a pony is that it should be pronounceable. Before the final selection write the name on a piece of paper and ask a variety of people to say it aloud.

Dry shampoos sold in pharmacies for patients who cannot wash their hair can be used on ponies. This is particularly helpful in the winter months. Be prepared, however, for some puzzled looks if you walk away from the counter with half a dozen bottles tucked under your arm.

If you are stabling at the showgrounds, take a few bright lightbulbs. We found that the lightbulbs in the barns tend to be too dim or burned out.

If a velvet hat gets wet, first steam it and then rub it hard with a towel.

Do not expect *all* of your children to fall in love with the barn. When we say that our five-year-old learned to ride at Hobby Horse Farm we are referring to his dirt bike.

When traveling home from shows on a Sunday night make sure that your children's duffel bags with school books and clothes are in your car and not in the car they rode to the show in at 4 AM. In fact, always check your belongings at the end of the show. Leave-taking always seems markedly hurried; tempers are short, children tired, and mothers totally exhausted. It is easy to leave things behind. The staff at a large *A* show once found a pony that had been forgotten.

Emptying the muck bucket

The Equine Eye

153

Beware of the temptation to use garbage bags as hold-all replacements. One HSM packed her child's belongings in a garbage bag at the end of the show — Pytchley jacket, books, velvet hat, shirts, etc. Everything lying around the tack room at the end of the show went in the bag. And yes, the garbage was removed by some helpful person, never to be found despite a desperate search at the city dump.

Don't dry clean the show jacket too much. The finish becomes dull with frequent cleanings. Try putting it briefly in a cool dryer with a damp towel and then hang it up immediately. And invest in a good clothes brush.

Definitions

Green Horse Show Mothers — Mothers whose children have not shown prior to the first day of December of the previous year.

Cold back — This refers to a pony that, when a saddle is placed on its back or the girth tightened, reacts by rearing, bucking, etc. At winter shows the HSM has a cold back, cold front, cold feet . . .

Cooling off — If a pony is overheated, it must be walked to cool it off gradually; failure to cool the pony properly can lead to colic. HSMs need to cool off after a particularly bad day (failure to do so can lead to ulcers) or a very hot, humid day (when a motel with a pool is appreciated).

Seeing a distance — A rider can see the distance if she is able to find the exact spot where the pony should leave the ground. Such a rider is said to have a *good eye*.

Drenching — For the HSM it's the soaking she receives during a storm. For a pony it's the liquid (usually medicine) given by lifting its head and pouring it down the throat.

Turn out — This can refer to the way that the rider and pony are dressed and groomed, or putting the pony in a paddock to run free.

Sticking a pony — When you determine the height of a pony with a measuring stick, you are said to stick the pony. This also refers to hitting the pony with a crop.

Off their feed — When ponies (or humans) do not eat their respective meals they are said to be off their feed. This can be a result of illness, nerves, heat . . .

Pulling the mane — This refers to removing hairs from the under-side of the mane, making it easier to braid.

Fittings — When the HSM purchses a new saddle she quickly finds out that the fittings include the stirrup leathers, stirrups, and girth — which are not usually included in the purchase price of the saddle.

154

HSM studying the "order to go"

JUMPING ORDER

Class No.	GREEN PONIES Horse's No. & Name	No.	SMALL PONIES Horse's No. & Name
1	239 Silent Promise	26	28 Festive Smile
2	98 Amelia Benolia	27	163 Snowslide
3	127 Glanmart Opal	28	39 Just Call Me Sir
4	27 Diamond Gem	29	249 Buttons & Bows
5	237 Who's the Boss	30	72 Frankly Alarming
6	121 Love a Lot	31	237 Who's the Boss
7		32	
8		33	28 Medium Hunter Pocket Star
9	Small Junior	34	16 Foxy Lady
10	213 Kilts	35	133 Sunshine
11		36	

"Order to go"

155

Chasing points — This refers to trying to accumulate as many points as possible so that a pony can either qualify for the indoor shows or place high in the horse-of-the-year standings sponsored by the AHSA.

The indoor shows — The big fall shows held at Madison Square Garden in New York City, the Pennsylvania National Horse Show in Harrisburg, the Royal Winter Fair in Toronto, and the Washington International are referred to as the indoor shows. Exhibitors must qualify in order to compete.

Muck out — Cleaning out a stall by removing the droppings and wet bedding. The HSM may be astounded by the child who mucks out her pony's stall with a fervor and fastidiousness never displayed when cleaning her own room.

Independent seat — This refers to the rider who can remain balanced on the pony's back without using the stirrups or reins.

Independent rider — When the child can compete without her HSM in attendance.

Natural aids — The means of communication between the rider and pony: hands, legs, voice, and body.

Artificial aids — The means of communication between the rider and pony: crop, spurs . . .

Mother's aids — These include the natural aids (hands, legs, voice, and body) which function as a means of communication between the HSM ad her competitors. They also include the tips found throughout this book.

Equine eye — At the large shows you can sign up for the Equine Eye which checks the ponies hourly throughout the night. But to the HSM the equine eye is on you. So behave. Gossip is part of what makes the horse show world go round; better someone else than you.

Order to go — This is not a burger, fries and a coke, but refers to the order in which the riders and ponies compete in an over fences class.

Made pony — Well-trained and experienced ponies are referred to as made.

Sizes — Small, medium and large won't cover it. So before you shop for child or pony, ask the trainer what size to get: what size bit . . . what size cooler . . . what size jodhpur straps . . . what size leathers . . . what size stirrups . . . what size martingale . . . what size bit . . . and what size pony.

DISCOVER
THE HOWELL
EQUESTRIAN LIBRARY

Because pleasure horses are an important part of your life, the fine books listed here deserve an important place in your library. Here are books of uncompromising excellence on every aspect of horses as recreation. This list includes many outstanding books you should own, so today discover the HOWELL EQUESTRIAN LIBRARY and get more out of the horses that mean so much to you.

ATHLETIC HORSE, The
Carol Foster
ISBN O-87605-858-6

BASIC GUIDE TO HORSE
CARE & MANAGEMENT
Bruce Mills & Barbara Carne
ISBN O-87605-871-3

DRESSAGE: AN APPROACH
TO COMPETITION
Kate Hamilton
ISBN O-87605-862-4

EDUCATING HORSES FROM
BIRTH TO RIDING
Peter Jones
ISBN O-87605-854-3

EQUINE INJURY & THERAPY
Mary Bromiley
ISBN O-87605-864-0

EQUINE VETERINARY MANUAL
Tony Pavord & Rod Fisher
ISBN O-87605-863-2

FESTIVAL OF DRESSAGE, A
Jane Kidd
ISBN O-87605-859-4

FOALING: BROOD MARE & FOAL
MANAGEMENT
Ron & Val Males
ISBN O-87605-851-9

GOOD MUDDER'S GUIDE, The
*Cheryl M. Seaver &
Laura J. Cunningham*
ISBN O-87605-875-6

GUIDE TO RIDING & HORSE CARE
Elaine Knox-Thompson & Suzanne Dickens
ISBN O-87605-852-7

HORSE & HORSEMANSHIP, The
Tamas Flandorffer & Jozsef Hajas
ISBN 963-13-1643-2

HORSE CARE, COMPLETE BOOK OF
Tim Hawcroft, B.V.Sc (Hons) M.A.C.I .Sc.
ISBN O-7018-1518-3

HORSES ARE MADE TO BE HORSES
Franz Mairinger
ISBN O-87605-855-1

LESS-THAN-PERFECT HORSE, The
Jane Thelwall
ISBN O-87605-872-1

LONG DISTANCE RIDING
Marcy Drummond
ISBN O-87605-861-6

PASTURE MANAGEMENT FOR
HORSES & PONIES
Gillian McCarthy
ISBN O-87605-865-9

PERFORMANCE HORSE, The:
MANAGEMENT, CARE & TRAINING
Sarah Pilliner
ISBN O-87605-856-X

RIDING CLASS
British Horse Society
ISBN O-87605-860-8

SHOWJUMPING
John Smart
ISBN O-87605-868

SYSTEMS OF THE HORSE
*Jeremy Houghton Brown &
Vincent Powell-Smith*
ISBN-O-87605-866-7

TICKNER'S HORSES
John Tickner
ISBN O-948253-09-6

TICKNER'S LIGHT HORSE
John Tickner
ISBN O-87605-874-8

YOUNG HORSE, The
*Elaine Knox Thompson &
Suzanne Dickens*
IBN O-87605-857-8

YOUNG RIDER'S GUIDE
TO HORSE & PONY CARE, A
Jane Kidd
ISBN O-87605-870-5